LET CHILDREN BE

a collection of stories

compiled by
Pippa Murray & Jill Penman

Thanks to Barrow Cadburys for their generous sponsorship without which this book would not have been possible.

Thanks to all those friends who have helped us in many different ways – with inspiration, advice, encouragement, listening, proof-reading and child-care.

Particular thanks to Len Barton, Dave Hampshire and Philip Roddis.

Published by:
ibk initiatives
Aizlewood's Mill
Nursery Street
Sheffield S3 8GG
Email: info@ibkinitiatives.com
www.ibkinitiatives.com

© ibk initiatives
Reprinted December 1996 and January 2008
ISBN 0 952 6864 0 6

Book Design & Layout by Dave Hampshire
Illustrations for cover & section dividers by Jessie Murray
Printed by Impact Graphics

For all our children

CONTENTS

ii   Acknowledgments
vii Introduction

1 Setting the Scene
   2   The Journey
   3   When you look at my child
   5   Life

7 Stories of Exclusion
   8   Just another routine hospital appointment
   9   A valued place in society
  10 V.E. Day
  11 Kim
  12 Why Mainstream is not enough
  15 Starting in Reception – Still in Reception
  17 Some thoughts after yet another meeting
  19 Learning from experience

25 Stories of Inclusion
  26 Facilitation
  27 Chris
  28 Exclusion/Inclusion
  30 Marsha
  33 Class Six
  34 Jenny's First Term at School
  37 Sam
  38 Blake
  41 Friendships
  42 Dear Annie
  44 Dear Bethan
  47 Bethan

48 An Ordinary Life
50 My kind of community
52 Wise and visionary teachers

55 *Stories of Professionals*
56 Sylvia
63 My child
65 Becoming different
68 To be continued
73 At what cost to our children
74 Hospitality
75 Dear Doctor
77 Let our children be

79 *Stories of Brothers And Sisters*
82 My brother and me
85 Dear Bethan
86 For Lily
88 Lily
89 Dinner
90 The future is assured
93 Kim
94 SNAG Parents Group
95 Contributors to the Collection

INTRODUCTION

This is a collection of stories. Some stories like these have already been told. We know there are many more stories waiting to be uncovered. This collection contributes to a bigger picture. It is important that such stories are heard. So often the discrimination our children face is not seen and not understood.

What is of great importance to us is that all our children are accepted by and belong in their local communities. We want them all to have friends, to be valued, to make contributions, to join in with things that are going on and so on. We would like all of our children to be treated as ordinary children – as the individuals they are. All children should belong in this way, shouldn't they?

Our disabled children are often not accepted as the individuals they are but are given labels and categories instead that can make it difficult for them to be accepted, and can prevent them from easily belonging. They have to struggle hard to enjoy ordinariness and we have to work hard to protect the bits of belonging that are happening.

For us the concept of segregation is completely unjustifiable.
It is morally offensive. It contradicts any notion of civil liberties and human rights –whoever it is done to, wherever it appears. Segregation is damaging for our children, for our families and for our communities. We do not want our children to be sent to segregated schools or any other form of segregated provision. We do not want our children and our families to be damaged in this way. Our communities should not be impoverished by the loss of our children.

This is a collection of stories from families who have been part of each others' journey, in one way or another. We are very pleased our children have brought us together. We value these connections greatly
It is to each other that we look for support, encouragement, inspiration and empowerment.

We put this collection together with many thoughts in mind.

We wanted to record the struggles of our children. It is they and all other children in similar situations who will make things happen. They are pioneering the future.

We wanted to share these stories with other parents. We have met parents who tell us that they would not have known that their children could go to their local schools and stay in their communities had they not come across such stories. Some of these parents have gone on to demand ordinary rights for their own children. May many more parents do likewise.

We wanted to publicise more widely the current discrimination our disabled children face in their daily lives. Many people really do not realise what happens to our children. It can only help to have such stories become more public.

We wanted to put this collection together because we needed to. We live with our children and our families being treated badly on a daily basis. This hurts. The process of writing and then sharing some of this has been empowering. It has helped us continue on the journey of trying to live our lives as we choose.

This is a collection of stories about our lives. We have stories from our disabled children, from their brothers and sisters and from parents. Contributions are varied and diverse. They all reflect the theme of the collection, "Let our children be". They have come about in many different ways. Some appear to be obvious, others maybe not so. In some cases a person's very being and teaching has prompted a piece to be written. We have tried to acknowledge all contributions. Every contribution is important to the collection –every contribution is of equal value.

We are learning that the journey begins in our homes – in our own lives. We are learning to challenge the set of beliefs we grew up with. We are learning about being allies to our disabled children.

We write from a human rights perspective. We do not accept the medical or charitable models of disability which present our children as defective. These are the models we, as parents, are expected to accept and collude with against our children. To collude in this way would mean seeing our children in the negative way society at present sees

 *Introduction*

them. This would fundamentally damage our relationships with our children. It would fundamentally damage our families.

This is a collection of stories from our lives. It is not an attempt to present a comprehensive picture of parents' experience. Nor is it an attempt to present a comprehensive picture of difference. In these respects we are aware that there are many gaps. This collection only attempts to present an exploration of what we are learning from our lives about being allies to our disabled children.

Some of the stories are unnamed. Some are very personal and parents have not wanted their families to be identified. Others describe current situations where parents have not felt able to identify themselves for fear of identifying the situations involved. Parents often have to live with and manage very difficult relationships with professionals.
In our experience many professionals at present do not recognise and acknowledge the power they have and beyond that, the power they assume. The fact that some of the stories in this collection are unnamed reflects this.

Looking back at our journey so far we know that we have made mistakes along the way. No doubt we will look back at this publication in the future and be aware of the mistakes we are making now. This publication represents our thinking at the present time. We have a long way to go. We look forward to the journey ahead.

Our children are the ones who teach us about the issues. They give us the opportunities to learn and understand. They give us determination and confidence. They give us hope and courage. They show us how it can be.

Our children are teaching us how to be their allies. We're presenting this collection as allies to our children.

This collection belongs to them.

Pippa Murray
Jill Penman

SETTING THE SCENE

> The truth is this: we do need you, not to be "experts" or managers of our lives, but to be friends, enablers and receivers of our "gifts" to you. We need you to admit cheerfully what you don't know, without shame; to ask us what we need before providing it, to lend us your physical strength when appropriate, to allow us to teach you necessary skills; to champion our rights, to remove barriers previously set in place, to return to us any power you may have had over our lives. We may also need you to remind us of our importance to the world, and to each other, at times of tiredness and discouragement.
> We can live without patronage, pity and sentimentality, but we cannot live without closeness, respect and cooperation from other people.
> Above all we need you to refuse to accept any "segregation" of one group of humans from another as anything else but an unacceptable loss for all concerned.
>
> *Micheline Mason*

M. Mason and R. Rieser, *Disability Equality in the Classroom: a Human Rights Issue*, ILEA 1990

THE JOURNEY

We are on a journey
We have no destination in mind.
We go where the journey takes us.
Being on the journey is where we want to be.

Sometimes we travel together.
Sometimes alone.
Sometimes we travel fast.
Sometimes slow.
Sometimes one teaches, one leads.
Sometimes the other.
Sometimes we need encouragement,
Energy.

We bring our own unique gifts
to the journey.
We always have hope.
We always have determination.
We always have vision.
We always find what we need
if we wait long enough,
if we open ourselves up to all possibilities.

We are on a journey
We have no destination in mind.
The journey goes on forever.
Being on the journey is where we want to be.

Pippa Murray
with thanks to Kim for giving me the words through his being

WHEN YOU LOOK AT MY CHILD

What do you see
When you look at my child?
How does he make you feel?

Your words confirm what I see in your eyes
Confident words, so secure
In the assumptions that you make.

Which child are you speaking about?

What do you see
When you look at me?
How do I make you feel?

Your manner suggests the response you expect
So sure of your words, taking
For granted the role that you choose.

Are you really talking to me?

When did I tell you I wanted him changed
That I would prefer him different
From as he is?
When did I tell you I wanted your help
To change him?
I longed for my child for such a long time
I met him and chose him
And held my breath for a while.
I was very lucky.
He decided I belonged to him too.

Why would I change him?

Don't you realise that I can feel
Your need to change him
Your need for him to be other than as he is
To be "improved"
To be more or less or whatever
You are disturbed by?

Don't you understand that
The comments you make about my child
Tell about yourself
And not about him?

And the needs we discuss
Are yours
And not his.

When you look at my child.

Jill Penman

Life

I am fifteen and I am different because I am fostered and I have learning difficulties. I have difficulties with spelling and reading. The reasons I have difficulty with spelling and reading are because I had a rough start in life being passed about between foster parents and children's homes and because I had a 30% hearing loss caused by "glue ear" until I was six. When I was five I moved to live with the foster parents I am still with. I started going to school regularly and got my ear fixed.

In infant school I had some good friends who were cleverer. The teacher found me difficult because I didn't like sitting still and I could not speak very well but I knew a lot of swear words.

In junior school my friend and I had special help. Some of the helpers did not know how to help us. One started to cry because we got fed up with her and we got into trouble. I got into trouble quite a lot still do but not so much.

When I left junior school I was sent to a special school. (I don't like that word "special" it should be a good word but it's been spoilt.) My mum and dad sent me there because they were worried that the local school would not cope with me.

To be honest I am not sure I would have lasted five minutes in my local school if I had gone there first of all because I messed about so much. I felt confused and got fed up because I could not read. The head from the special school still haunts me because I don't think he believed in me but my class teacher did, she was my friend and knew I could make it.

The head teacher was cross with me because he knew I had a good home and other kids at the school were in children's homes or had poor families, but he didn't understand I still had a lot to sort out about myself.

At special school I learned that people with Downs Syndrome or

Setting the Scene

disabilities are people the same as the rest of us and that people who take the mick out of them don't understand. If mainstream had all these people in then everyone would get used to them and understand more. The advantage was that there were more adults to help and not so many kids to share the equipment. I was really pleased when I moved to mainstream school. When I am having break with my friends I can forget that I cannot spell and read properly I'm the same as them then. They may be better than me at reading but I am better than some at practical things such as woodwork or cooking. Sometimes people are surprised how good I am. You can see the amazed expression in their faces.

My mum and dad had to fight for me to go into mainstream school and to get support for me to be able to be with my peer group. I do need someone to check my work with me and my brother and sisters have their uses.
When I first started at mainstream school I had loads of stick. The kids used to say did you go to "spasa" school and things like that. They didn't understand but now they don't call me names.

I like being with people of my own age and I can do all sorts of things with friends now like go to the night club and roller booting and I think I am learning o.k. I can read what I want in my fishing magazine and biking magazine.

I have learned how to read a sentence, stop and then read again so I can get the sense of it even if I can't read every word.

George Hawkins

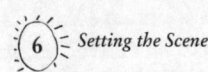
Setting the Scene

> The medical model of disability sees the disabled person as the problem. We are to be adapted to fit into the world as it is. If this is not possible, then we are shut away in some specialised institution or isolated at home, where only our most basic needs are met. The emphasis is on dependence, backed up by the stereotypes of disability that call forth pity, fear and patronising attitudes. Usually the impairment is focused on, rather than the needs of the person. The power to change us seems to lie within the medical and associated professions, with their talk of cures, normalisation and science. Often our lives are handed over to them.

Richard Rieser

M. Mason and R. Rieser, *Altogether Better (From 'Special Needs' to Equality in Education)*, Hobsons Publishing, 1994

JUST ANOTHER ROUTINE HOSPITAL APPOINTMENT

It was a lovely balmy summers day in 1965 and I decided we would walk through the park to the hospital, enjoy the sun. 'A' was in her pram looking very pretty in her little cotton dress and sun bonnet. She was over the life-threatening episodes of pneumonia she had suffered in her first years of life, the plastic surgery operation on her ears was successful and she was to have a "frog splint" to cure her congenital hip dislocation.

'A' was gaining weight and looking very bonny. The routine visit to the doctor went well. 'A' was OK but would we like to go and see the almoner. Off we went. We were invited into her office and offered a chair.

There was a vacancy at the local mental handicap hospital and 'A' could be admitted that day, the almoner was prepared to take us now, we were lucky to be offered this opportunity as places did not come up very often and with 'A' in the hospital I could go home and have another baby. I declined her offer. I had a baby. 'A' was the one I wanted, not another one. The almoner was not pleased. She had gone to a lot of trouble on my behalf and I was not to forget that 'A' wasn't going to be like other children, she would be a cabbage and lie in her cot all day. 'A' would never know who I was, she would never walk, talk or go to school and she was not expected to live very long. I still refused. I was unceremoniously ushered out of the office bewildered, grief stricken and very very angry.

name withheld

A VALUED PLACE IN SOCIETY?

In the past, as now, the more disabled the person, the fewer the choices. Few, if any services and no allowances were available to help people stay in their community, cared for at home. When families were no longer able to cope the disabled person inevitably went into a mental handicap hospital. This happened to 'A'.

These hospitals were "warehouses for people" with minimal care and absolutely no services geared to individual needs. The whole ten years 'A' was in hospital was a constant battle to keep a relationship going and to remind the staff she was my daughter, not just a patient.

I now relate the most traumatic and telling experience of all those wasted years.

'A' spent her weekdays at school and her weekends at home with the family. One Friday afternoon we went to collect 'A' but she was too ill to come home, the doctor had been and antibiotics had been prescribed. 'A' was never to receive them as when they were delivered they were put in the office, which closed at 5pm on Friday and did not open till 9am on Monday. No one in the hospital had a key.

'A' got progressively worse over the weekend and we were unaware that she was not getting her medicine. Laryngitis had now turned to pneumonia.

On Sunday pm as we walked into the ward the local GP was standing at 'A's bed and saying to the charge nurse,

"Keep her comfortable but she will be gone for tomorrow."

The charge nurse was nodding, acquiescing. I opened my mouth to protest but nothing came out. Fortunately for 'A' 'D', her stepfather, was with me and looking the GP straight in the eye said,

"If she dies I'll see you in the coroner's court."

One hour later 'A' was in hospital, hooked up to a drip, very very ill. Five weeks later she came home, thin, pale but alive. She's still here fifteen years on.

name withheld

V.E. Day

I've been sitting watching the V.E. day celebrations on the television. One beacon was lit in Wales to remember the children in Europe who didn't survive or who were permanently scarred by the war. This set off my tears for the children who the Nazi regime described as "useless eaters", children, disabled, probably very much like my child. These were the children who were the first group to be exterminated as they were relatively easily seen as "not fully human". They were used to get people used to killing other people who didn't fit the "norm", or who were seen as "different".

If celebrations about peace are to mean anything at all, our movement and struggle for total inclusion for EVERYONE is VITAL. It is only when our children, along with all other children, are fully included everywhere, that there will be safety for any of us in the future.

Caroline MacKeith

Kim

When I first had Kim he was my son.
A year later he was epileptic and developmentally delayed.
At eighteen months he had special needs and he was a special child. He had a mild to moderate learning difficulty. He was mentally handicapped.

I was told not to think about his future.

I struggled with all this.

By the time he was four he had special educational needs.
He was a statemented child. He was dyspraxic, epileptic, developmentally delayed and had complex communication problems.

Two years later, aged six, he was severely epileptic (EP), cerebral palsied (CP) and had complex learning difficulties.

At eight he had severe intractable epilepsy with associated communication problems. He was showing a marked developmental regression. He had severe learning difficulties.

At nine he came out of segregated schooling and he slowly became my son again. Never again will he be anything else but Kim – a son, a brother, a friend, a pupil, a teacher, a person.

Pippa Murray

WHY MAINSTREAM IS NOT ENOUGH

Four years ago, when my son was in a segregated school for children labelled as having severe learning difficulties, there was nothing appropriate for him to do in the classroom. I sent in books and puzzles.

Last week, when my son was in his local mainstream school where he is now a part-time pupil, there was nothing appropriate for him to do in the classroom. I sent in books and puzzles.

Four years ago, when my son was in a segregated school he sat through the music lessons disinterested and choosing not to participate. From time to time a teacher or assistant would take his hands, place a triangle and beater in them, and tap the beater to the triangle. This was meant to be my son participating, making music. His face was blank, his eyes distant.

Last week, when my son was in his local mainstream school he sat through the music lessons disinterested and choosing not to participate. His support worker looked at the worksheet all the children had been given and copied down the answers for my son. This was meant to be my son participating in the music lesson. His face was blank, his eyes distant.

Four years ago, when my son was in a segregated school, there was a drama lesson. My son sat on the floor, three adults waved a sheet over his head – this was the wind. Then his teacher sprayed water on to his face – this was the rain. My son screamed – not liking the cold water sprayed senselessly on to his face. He sat and watched as the other children experienced the same fate. This was meant to be my son participating in the drama lesson. His face was blank, his eyes distant.

Last week, when my son was in his local mainstream school, there was a drama lesson. My son sat on a chair. His support worker pretended that my son, who speaks very little – choosing to communicate in other ways – did not speak English and that she was his interpreter. She

Stories of Exclusion

interpreted his imaginary speech into English. This was meant to be my son participating in the drama lesson. His face was blank, his eyes distant.

Four years ago, when my son was in a segregated school, I went into school and talked with his teacher and head-teacher. I was unhappy about the experience he was having at school, worried about the lack of anything that caught his imagination or interest. I was concerned that little was being done to foster relationships between my son and his classmates. As I voiced my concerns I watched their faces change – they felt threatened and defensive. At the end of the meeting they said they could not change the school for one pupil. I took my child out of school.

Last week, when my son was in his local mainstream school I went into school and talked with his support teacher. I was unhappy about the experience he was having at school, worried about the lack of anything that caught his imagination or interest. I was concerned that little was being done to foster relationships between my son and his classmates. As I voiced my concerns I watched his face change – he felt threatened and defensive. At the end of the meeting he said he was surprised at my comments, parents of other "special needs" children were so grateful to them. He did not understand my concerns. I left school, determined to make the experience better for my son, but unsure as to what I should do next, how I could make it better for him.

Last week the support teacher and support worker at my son's local mainstream school visited the teacher at the segregated school. They wanted ideas about how to teach my son. They talked about my son's "inability to communicate" with others – especially the other children in his class. They decided that the teacher from the segregated school would come up to the local mainstream school and would – with my approval which was assumed as given – teach the support worker a specialised communication system. The support worker would then spend an hour a week teaching my son – taking him away from his classmates to do so. She would then teach the other children in his class. My son would then, magically, be able to communicate with his classmates in an acceptable way. He would, in their eyes, have made good progress.

Last week I voiced my concerns about this plan. I spoke of the need to start with my son. To look at the way he chooses to communicate and encourage that. To find things that interest him and explore those with his classmates. I asked what would happen if my son was not interested in this communication system – would he be seen to have failed –again? It was noted that once again I was questioning professional opinion, obstructing any attempts made to help my son. My words went unheard, my voice of knowledge and experience of my son was not listened to.

We persevere because my son has a right to belong in his community, to have a place at his local mainstream school. We persevere because my son has a right to equal opportunity; we are fighting for his civil rights.

We struggle every day. I wonder about the price we pay, especially the price my son pays, for our perseverance. I wonder how long we can go on paying such a high price.

name withheld

 Stories of *Exclusion*

STARTING IN RECEPTION...
STILL IN RECEPTION...

When James started at his local school he was in the Reception class and we as parents were pleased he was to be with other children of the same age.

Our opportunities to meet other parents were limited. James only attended on a part-time basis, which meant we missed the informal contact with other parents at 'going home time'. We made every effort to get to know the children and parents. We attended Home/School meetings and went on class days out whenever we could. James was invited to birthday parties and invited his friends to his party. Some of the children clearly liked him, and he liked some of them. The result of the efforts we made were some good relationships with some other parents and some friendships for James which included visits for tea. Lovely, ordinary stuff.

When the time came for James' class to move out of Reception we were told he would not be moving with them. What about his friendships, we asked. His relationships were not 'significant ones', a teacher said. Her ignorant words still hurt us two years later. Throughout James' time at the school we have had to compromise, weighing the many advantages of his being there against poor practice. So, encouraged by meeting the Reception teacher for the coming year, we compromised.

James started his second Reception and had to make a whole new set of friends. Our opportunities to meet other parents were still restricted as he still attended on a part-time basis. We attended Home/School meetings and went on class days out whenever we could. The round of birthday parties produced some invitations. Some of the children liked James, and James liked some of the children. The result of our efforts were some good relationships with some other parents and some friendships for James including visits for tea. Lovely, ordinary stuff.

When the time came for this class to move James was to move with them at last. Within a few weeks we were told it was 'not working' in

Stories of Exclusion

the new class. The 'answer' was to return him to Reception.

He is still there.

Our opportunities to meet another set of parents remain restricted but, frankly, we do not want to get to know another set – nothing personal, you understand, but why should we? One or two of the children have invited James to their parties, which is a delight, but we fully understand why the frequency has dropped. He is two years older than the rest of the class – and about a foot taller. He has made some friends in this class, but why should he have to? James has few words but tries very hard to engage with other children. He wants to be friends, to be included. Instead of being able to keep and develop his original class friendships he has had to start from scratch again and again.

name withheld

Some Thoughts After Yet Another Meeting

We went to a meeting recently which was part of a piece of research in the city about people's ideas of community in relation to schools and school systems – looking to the future. We thought it might be interesting, maybe encouraging; that it might be a place to make contacts, an opportunity to share ideas, perhaps even visions of what might be.

The discussion touched on many issues – the nature of community, the people and groups involved, the relationship between community and schools, the needs communities have of their schools.

People shared ideas they felt to be important. We had the opportunity to make points about all children belonging in their local communities and school, being of equal value, being included. Other people made comments about access, attitude, equity. It was good to see people generally nodding and giving the impression of support and agreement for such ideas.

The discussion moved on. Comments were made about some types of school not being available locally, the need for a range of provision to cover all needs, the need for choice in terms of types of provision. Many of the people who had nodded at the previous statements were nodding at these ones too.

And very soon we heard that "of course more children could probably cope with mainstream" but they were "talking about the severe ones"; that "there would always be a need for some special schools for these youngsters"; that "the local community they worked in just would not be able to cope with such children". The same predictable things: the labels, the prejudice and discrimination, the anxieties and fears.

How can it be possible to agree that all children have the right to belong and be included in local communities and at the same time state that some should be segregated? Surely it's a contradiction unless somehow our children are not perceived as children after all; are not

Stories of Exclusion

really perceived as human beings, but as less than human – and therefore don't count. It seems that all children should be of equal value, except children with disability labels.

So, just to make it clear – all children are of equal value. No school can claim to meet the needs of its community until all the children in its neighbourhood are included and positively supported by right.

And just to make it perfectly clear – all means all.

Jill Penman

Learning from Experience

Julie is our oldest child. She was born in 1958 when the world was a very different place and we were different people. Julie was a beautiful baby and also our first born. We were proud and happy parents.

I was a regular in the R.A.F. and of necessity we lived away from our families. We were posted to Cyprus when Julie was seven months old and life was pretty good.

Months passed by and because we were new and inexperienced parents we were not aware that Julie's developmental progress was delayed in many respects. We finally realised that all was not well and began the rounds of doctors and specialists. It was a demoralising process which lasted two years.

In those days consultants were like superior beings from a different planet. None of them would tell us anything and Julie received a course of treatment for a non-existent disability which turned out to be completely inappropriate.

We were so distressed and angered by those events that I risked court martial by telling the consultant very bluntly what I thought of him, and demanded our return to England so that we could find out what was wrong with Julie.

I wasn't court martialled and we did come home. Val was in the final stages of pregnancy with our eldest son by the time we finally got an appointment at the Sheffield Children's Hospital. I took Julie along for a series of tests and returned home some time later for a diagnosis and prognosis.

The diagnosis and prognosis was what I now know to be the classic horror story of those times.

"Your child has massive brain damage. She will be a cabbage and you should think about placing her in full time care."

Many years later we found that Julie's disabilities were caused either at birth through lack of oxygen or at six months due to an adverse reaction to a smallpox vaccination.

At the time we were shown no humanity or even empathy. There was no positive counselling, no support system or services. We were stunned, emotionally devastated and made to feel guilty and worthless. Julie was still a happy, loving, beautiful child and she now had a brother so we simply got on with our lives and tried not to think too far into the future.

We were living on the borders of three counties by the time Julie reached school age. Our contact with Education Services was brief. They simply said that Julie was ineducable.

We did seek help and were put in touch with a day centre in a local town. Julie had a three day trial and was rejected as being in need of more support than they could provide. We were told yet again that Julie needed full time "specialist care".

We got on with our lives. I am sure that Val and I thought a lot about the future but I don't recall talking about it much. I had a mixture of emotions which included "why me?", guilt, helplessness, pain, anger and isolation.

I was posted to Aden in 1964. The R.A.F. said it was not possible for us to take Julie and a welfare officer was drafted in to help us decide what to do. All of the services we were put in contact with, voluntary as well as statutory, recommended the same thing:

"Julie needs full-time residential care. It will be her only chance of developing her full potential, and will provide her with the best specialist care."

We were a disciplined and believing lot in those days. We expected experts to know what they were talking about, and accepted their advice. Julie lived in hospitals for twenty years because of that. Times have changed, thank goodness!

Giving Julie to the "experts", in what we believed to be her best interests, was the most painful thing I have ever experienced. I stayed strong and rational on the outside and was in total turmoil inside.

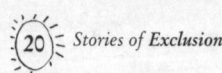

Stories of Exclusion

That's what men did in those days.

Julie continued to be a part of our lives throughout those years, but a special, extraordinary part. She came home for visits, we visited her. When we were stationed abroad other family members visited her and one of us came home every six months to spend a fortnight's holiday with her. She gained two more brothers in that time who had not known her as an integral, every day part of the family.

Many people who lived in those hospitals with Julie didn't have any visitors. I am sure that their families must have shared my feelings of guilt and helplessness to such an extent that they had to bury them and abandon those relatives. Such was the power of the "expert" advice of those times.

I will not dwell on the reality of life in an institution – that has been researched to the nth degree. Suffice it to say it did not "cure" Julie or give her any better opportunities. It simply distanced her from those people who most loved and cared about her, or would have done given the chance.

Because Julie resided in institutions and we lived in many different places we did not become members of any advocacy organisations such as Mencap.

We were set in aspic of the "system" and unaware of campaigns, for example to establish a right to education for everyone. It was a pleasant surprise when Julie started school at thirteen, even though it was on the hospital site.

The years passed and we maintained our established routine. We became aware that people were talking about Care in the Community and hospital closures in the early 'eighties. Nobody likes changes so my immediate reaction was: you can't close my daughter's home, followed by: but the experts said…, followed by: don't trust the ******s, – we'll find out for ourselves and make up our own minds.

By 1984 Julie was back home. We had been central to the formation of an "Action Group" and were taking the experts to task. Heady days!

Since 1984 Julie has had many experiences. Some have been positive, wonderful, magic and unexpected.

For example:
- Becoming simply Julie Molloy rather than a list of labels.
- Worthwhile but difficult reconnection to her family, which now includes a nephew and two nieces.
- A short term befriender called Cathy who took her out on the student scene to pubs, theatres, burger joints and discos.
- People in the Services who enabled her to abseil in a wheelchair, canoe, yacht, horse ride and many other things.
- Hard won general medical and specialist treatment for basic health care, including rheumatoid arthritis and diabetes.

And some have been negative and challenging. For example:
- Reconnection to family and community as just "Julie" and ordinary after years of being "special".
- Teaching GPs that she needs ordinary medical treatment rather than tranquillisers.
- Being perceived as "special needs", "food for jobs" and subject to long established custom and practice by some workers in this fair but extremely demarcated city.
- Realising how many people are excluded from ordinary society because of their condition, race, beliefs or disability.

Julie is a survivor and quietly strong. She has had to tolerate many bad situations, challenges and barriers. She has done so with a fortitude which would win medals at the Olympics. She enjoys life and meanwhile we seek the Holy Grail situation which will enable her to continue to do so when we are not around.

We have been involved in many forms of advocacy and believe that we have learned a lot from the life experience of Julie and many other people like her.

I have changed my view of Julie from someone who can only be cared for and controlled by experts, to seeing her as an individual person who has rights, including the right to be included in the everyday happenings and opportunities of society and the community.

 *Stories of* **Exclusion**

Perhaps the best description of what we have tried to achieve with Julie after all the wasted years is provided by the following advice from Dr Wolf Wolfensberger, the architect of Citizen Advocacy and a leading figure in designing the philosophy of Human Services in the USA and elsewhere.

He says that parents can be very effective allies to their children by acting on the following advice:

1. Make sure that we maintain, strengthen and renew the family ties around our sons and daughters. If they are to be regarded as individual human beings who have identity and value, rather as a bundle of needs called "handicapped", the family is the place to start.

2. Explain the reality of existence in an "institution" to family members and anyone else who will listen.

3. Make sure your son/daughter is included in whatever groups and activities you take part in. Don't be put off by the occasional bad experience. Get people to relate to, understand and accept him/her as a person.

4. Make sure whatever advice your son/daughter receives improves his/her acceptance as a member of society.

5. Help each other by mutual aid and support.

6. Join and support the organisations which defend and promote your son/daughter's best interests.

7. Encourage the creation of a Citizen Advocacy Office in your area. (We have one of high repute in Sheffield.)

8. Make it your top priority to encourage positive, personal, voluntary relationships for your son/daughter.

9. Make sure that services are designed and provided in ways which enhance and promote their value as members of the community with rights.

These give an outline of the many ways in which you can be an effective ally to your son or your daughter. We have travelled a long journey through many service philosophies over many years, before we decided to think for ourselves.

Our experience is that parents can, and it works!

Vince, Val & Julie Molloy

> The nature of our work, my many friends and I, is first of all to imagine the world of inclusion. The world is not real! It is a dream – an ancient dream to be sure, but nevertheless a dream. It is simply a human dream of the world where equality is not an issue because difference is not an issue. It speaks of a world where difference and diversity are radically resourceful; where everything that is done or built is created out of the gift of opportunity that diversity provides. It is the world where exclusion is essentially unthinkable because to exclude anyone would be to rob the community of its most precious resource – the opportunity that that person's difference makes possible.

Judith Snow

Enchantment for Inclusion, in Learning Together *Magazine, Issue 4, March 1993*

Facilitation

Caroline: "What do you think about facilitated communication?"
Maresa: "GOOD!"

I've always known that Maresa understands well.

For years I've watched her eyes, her face, her body, her tension, her relaxation, her humour.

Why don't other people understand?

I've felt so bad that I couldn't give Maresa a means to tell me just what she wanted, or what she thought, but at least I knew I didn't know how, and was willing to learn. Not so most "experts" who, because they thought they knew, were incapable of learning.

People said to me, "but it's no more difficult than with babies before they can speak!"

How can they say that: she's three, four, five, six, seven, eight – then how wonderful.

Somebody came who did understand. Maresa spelt the answers to her questions. She had been teaching herself to read.

O tears of Joy and more Joy. For the next few weeks we felt our problems were over. They could be.

Except for the "special" teachers who still don't understand and don't want to learn. Except for people who don't want to wait. Our problems could be over except for a world that doesn't want to include Maresa's wonderful insights on its agenda.

But there are glimpses, usually unexpected. People can enjoy each other so, and some just do. It's all potentially there.

The Inclusion and then the understanding.

Caroline & Maresa MacKeith

Stories of Inclusion

CHRIS

My best friend Chris in Australia has a disability called Cerebral Palsy and Epilepsy. He uses a laptop to help him with his work and he has to take a tablet two times a day. Some people at school used to bully him. So he got fed up with them and decided to make a speech to tell them about cerebral palsy and what it does to him. People went up to him afterwards and apologised for what they had done and said about him. I thought he was very brave to do that and he shouldn't have had to. His disability had never made any difference to us.

Freddy Morrison

Exclusion

People at a conference were asked to think of two situations - one where they belonged and were included, the other where they were left out and excluded - and asked to record how it had made them feel, using marks, words, drawings, etc.

These are some of the comments made. We just show some of the words used - it was not possible to reproduce the drawings.

SNAG Parents Group: 'Inclusive Education' Conference, March 1994, Sheffield

Frightened, Lonely, Can't take anything in.

Empty, angry, unhealthy

Different, stressed, afraid, unloved, unhappy, unconfident, ridiculed, withdrawn, angry, prejudiced against.

not belonging, inadequate, unhappy, isolated

Insecure, stupid, failure, Low self esteem, Different.

Useless, unwanted, depressed, lonely, isolated

Like an outsider, felt confused, unhappy and unsure of myself

Unfair, frustrated

Lost, unwanted, lack of direction and focus, sadness, emptiness

Sad, angry, frustrated, part of conversation when I can't follow and contribute

Angry - wanting to change it

embarrassed, stupid, powerless, anxious

Worthless, cold, unimportant, unwanted, unpopular

Angry and upset, why have I been singled out? Not valued for who I am.

Hurt, dismayed, confused, angry, betrayed

cheated, disappointed, resigned, sad

Isolated, unhappy, unconfident, lonely

Sad, angry, hurt. Why and how can anybody behave like that?, isolation, What did I do to deserve that?

Frightened, angry, depressed, anxious

Cold, hate, horrible, mean, spiteful, bullying, lonely

Inclusion

Comfort.
Reinforcement that I was right.
Happiness
I had something to contribute.
Valued.

not frightened, safe, calm, hopeful, light hearted

comfortable
happy
relaxed
interested
safe

Warm, secure.
Anything is possible

relaxed, involved, warm, comfortable, valued

wanted, worthy, secure, safe

happy, part of the crowd, empowered

important, self-worth, loved, respected, have something to offer, with friends

Loved, being valued, being part, feeling caring from other people I cared about.

doing things together

warmth, talking or communicating in other ways, fun, happy, enjoy sharing secrets, friends, love, laughter

Loved, wanted, important, happy

happy, fulfilled in every little event of life.

Feeling valued,
feeling wanted,
feeling of equality,
feeling that you have rights.

not alone, relief, comfort, sharing

strong, confident, real, alert, easy, human, trust, warm

happy, warmth, healthy, alive

welcome, wanted, valued

Feel relaxed, able to contribute.
Valued.

Warm, valued,
needed, loved, safe.
Part of something.
Able.
Creative.

MARSHA

I have a seven year old daughter called Marsha, who enjoys horse riding, swimming and going to school, especially the playtime and P.E. bits.

She loves going to her friends' parties, especially the ones with bouncy castles or at McDonalds.

Marsha has learning difficulties. She cannot walk, run, skip or dance. She cannot talk or sing. She wears nappies and has fits when she goes to bed.

Marsha attended a nursery for children seen as having severe learning difficulties. She went for one morning a week and had to travel to the other side of the city to get there. Marsha also went to our local play school with the friends she had known since being a baby.

I was uncomfortable and unhappy when Marsha went to the nursery, but no other option was offered her. I was just going to have to get used to the idea that she would not go to the same local nursery as her friends or go to the rising five class at our local school, as her sisters had done.

I dreaded the time when Marsha reached school age and would be expected to attend every day, leaving her friends to go to our school while she went across town to another.

I wanted to know when and how I was going to accept that Marsha had to be excluded from our community. When would I ever feel comfortable with that idea?

I asked other parents of disabled children. I met a group of parents who believed all children, however different they are, should be included in everyone else's life, should be included in the community, including that of their local school.

Yes, that made sense to me too.

I approached the head teacher of our infant school and asked if

*Stories of **Inclusion***

Marsha could attend school every afternoon, as she carried out an intensive therapy programme every morning at home, helped by dozens of volunteers.

The head teacher did not think it was fair to exclude a local child from the school either, and agreed that if Marsha had the support of a Child Care Assistant (CCA) she could be included on the school register.

After some negotiation with the Local Education Authority (LEA), and with the enthusiastic support of the head teacher, it was agreed that Marsha would start school alongside her friends from play school.

If, during Marsha's first weeks and months in school, anyone had difficulty accepting Marsha's place in school, they would have learned much from her classmates.

After a brief explanation from me about how Marsha's brain box was injured, I told the children that by watching them walk, talk, skip, jump, play, draw and paint, Marsha might learn how to do these things too.

Yes, they nodded. That seems fair enough.

"Anything you'd like to ask?" I said nervously to the sea of upturned faces as they sat cross legged on the carpet.

"Yes, yes", an arm shot up. "Have you seen that Teenage Mutant Ninja Turtle film?" It was no big deal having Marsha in their class.

Some teachers were apprehensive, maybe a little nervous. They had not had a child like Marsha in school before. They were big enough to admit this and ask me questions. "I just want you to include Marsha in every aspect of school life."

Their attitude was positive; they were willing to learn from me, from the CCA and, most important of all, from Marsha herself.

Marsha's CCA, Chris, has shown everyone how to make inclusion of a child with special needs a positive and successful experience. Chris's enthusiasm, energy and hard work with Marsha in school, her willingness to help and teach children and staff how easy it is to include Marsha, has made my daughter's time at infant school a huge success.

Marsha's current teacher is only in her second year of teaching. She was apprehensive, but supportive nevertheless, and enthusiastic about

Marsha's inclusion in her class. At Marsha's recent Annual Review she spoke of Marsha's positive effect on the rest of the class in these words:

"Marsha is a very popular member of the class, the children are caring and considerate towards her. Marsha brings out the best in them. Marsha has had an extremely positive impact upon one particular member of the class. This child had problems socialising with other children but has struck up a real friendship with Marsha. He helps to get her ready for P.E. and will only partner her in country dancing.
He also went to her birthday party. This was the first party invitation that he'd accepted since he was in Reception...

...I feel that Marsha has, and is, integrated well into a 'mainstream' class. She benefits from the stimulation that the other children provide and in return they benefit both personally and socially."

Already the same positive, enthusiastic and supportive approach is evident in the Junior School Marsha will hopefully go onto in September. At Marsha's recent review, no less than three members of staff came along, eager to learn about inclusion, and eager to show their support. If they approach Marsha's presence in their school with the same enthusiasm, and if they receive the same resources and support as the staff at the Infant School, then Marsha's Junior School days will be equally successful.

Lindsay Hanson

CLASS SIX

Marsha learns how it feels to belong in class six. She sees how her friends run, dance, jump, sing, shout, argue, chatter. She learns how it feels to have friends who play with you. She learns how it feels to be with people who share with you, who care about you, who send Christmas cards to you.
She learns about Ronald McDonald parties, Andy the Clown parties, Bouncy Castle parties.
She learns what it feels like to be included in the school choir, Christmas plays and school trips. Marsha learns how it feels to belong.

The children from Marsha's class learn about Marsha. They learn that not every child can run, dance, jump, shout. They learn that sometimes you have to communicate in a different way. They learn that just because a person can't do the things they do or act the way they act or sound the same as they sound, they still matter the way that Marsha matters, that they still count the way that Marsha counts.

They learn that Marsha too has feelings and that she too can be happy or sad. They learn how to care and to think about people other than themselves. They learn how to help and assist Marsha with her class work.

They learn how much harder Marsha has to try to do the wonderful things which they enjoy and take for granted. They learn how tough it must be, without being excluded from everyone's lives too.

Lindsay Hanson

JENNY'S FIRST TERM AT SCHOOL

So here we were after months (or was it years?) of phone calls, discussions and worry. Jenny was finally starting school. It was the same school her brother had started five years before – had I worried so much about him?
We walked down the path. Would she be able to cope with her lunch, could she change her shoes, would she sit quietly at story time, would the other children like her, would they accept her. Had I had the same worries five years ago? I couldn't remember. What would I be feeling at Christmas? Would I still have the same conviction that Jenny should be in a mainstream school?

My 'what if' thoughts were suddenly stopped in their tracks by a little girl who came bounding up to us with a loud 'hello Jenny'. Jenny did not answer her as usual but she went into school without tears or protests, and this has now been the same for six months.

I have many memories of Jenny's first term which I shall always treasure. Walking into the classroom and being told that Jenny has a boyfriend – said boyfriend then duly appeared and gave Jenny a big hug that she returned with gusto! The time Jenny's support worker described her as being 'part of the crowd'! This certainly seemed to be the case when she was one of a group that managed to get their feet stuck down a hole and ended up with sodden wellies, covered in mud from head to foot! What a joy it must be to be an infant teacher!

It probably is the 'events' that took place during the term that are most easily remembered. Birthday parties – "Jenny is always going to parties, Mum", her brother said. "It's not fair." She certainly was developing a hectic social life: could I keep up with her? One week she was a pirate, the next a cowboy. The usual comment I got when I picked her up and asked if she'd been OK was, "well I think so; I didn't really notice". When Jenny had her party at the Pizza Hut, she got stuck in with all the others making the pizza and covering the carpet with the usual debris!

Stories of Inclusion

Then there was singing at harvest, collecting the Christmas tree from Clipstone Forest, going to the pantomime — now that was something.
I went as a parent-helper, fifty reception children on a double decker bus! Samantha sat next to Jenny with her arm around her, Sam is one of Jenny's special friends, she spends a lot of time telling Jenny that she loves her.

I don't know how much of the pantomime Jen understood but she stayed in her seat for one and a half hours and enjoyed the music. I would never have dared to take her on my own. That was a lesson to me.

Perhaps the event that brought the tears to my eyes and a lump to my throat was the Christmas Play. Her teacher had asked me to help Jen memorise three lines that she was going to say with two other children, one being Sam. I could not imagine in a month of Sundays Jen being able to do this in front of other people, or knowing when to stand up or sit down, but there she was on the front row. Sam gave her a prod when to stand up and also told her when to sit down. The children also told her to "shhh" when she started to get fidgety. There I was experiencing and feeling the same emotions as all the other mums of five year olds when they see them in their first school Nativity Play.

Obviously, reading this you might say 'well what about the difficulties?' Well she cannot always sit still in story time or watching TV, or listening for a long period of time as she does not fully understand, but her teachers have developed strategies for dealing with this.
She did go through a period of saying 'no' very aggressively, but again with the support that she has they worked through it, and like many things it seemed to be a phase she was going through. At the end of term I asked with trepidation how the staff felt the first term had been. Perhaps the thing that meant the most was when they said she had been an 'asset' to the class, that she had brought out the best in the other children, that they all cared for and looked after her.
This was not the answer I had expected.

When we go to the shops or down to the park, Jenny is known. "Oh that's Jenny, she goes to my school".

Jen is very much part of her community (actually more than her mother is). She is accepted for who she is, and she feels secure. How do I know? After two days holiday she said at breakfast: "go to school today?"

Julie Dalton

Sam

me and sam play in the bath evry nite

he purs water on my head and I pur t on h shead

Joe 6

Joe Jenkinson

"The rascals are here - it's me and Sam."
    Joe; brother, aged six.

"Sam's the cutest four year old that I know."
    Calum; friend, aged six.

"Me and Sam are playing with all this stuff and we're loving it."
    Bradley; friend, aged four.

Paul & Agnes Jenkinson

Stories of Inclusion

Blake

As I sat down to write this story in a snatched moment of peace, the doorbell went. Annoyed at the interruption I went to the door. There was David, a boy from up the road.

"Is Blake playing today?"
"He's out now. But call back later, he'd love to play."

My annoyance was short lived. Although the local children coming round to ask if Blake is coming out to play is now common, it always thrills me. I shall never take it for granted. Blake is now nine. Five years ago I could never have imagined anyone calling round for Blake.

It seems that Blake and I have had struggles from the moment of his conception. My marital problems left me alone, pregnant and devastated. An odd pregnancy ended a month early with a blue, distressed baby who was so beautiful I couldn't take my eyes off him.

Days, weeks, months, years passed so slowly and yet in the blink of an eye. Blake at four years old was still a baby in nappies and a bib, yet so alert, so bright. The intensive programme we embarked on took over our lives but at last he started to learn. Whilst Blake would not be where he is now without the programme's input, it also creates other problems. An adult oriented environment, not enough male company, and too few opportunities for self expression.

Nursery was a godsend to us. Luckily, we live in a part of the city where the local school – head and staff – have vision, and were prepared to work to make Blake's placement a success.

Initially, despite the wholehearted support of the school, Blake's position seemed vulnerable. At every review there was always one professional who questioned the placement, one professional who brought up special school, one professional who would say Blake's

Stories of Inclusion

Joe Jenkinson

placement in mainstream could not be justified. I would come out of these reviews wondering what justification they were looking for. I would think about what was going on in the classroom and wonder that they could not see how everyone was benefiting from Blake being there.

Recently the class was having a silent reading period. Blake was sat reading his book in his lectern along with the rest of them. Suddenly a boy got up, not a close friend of Blake's, motioned to Blake to keep quiet and slipped to the back of the classroom. He rummaged in his

Stories of Inclusion

bag there, got out a magazine which had a beautiful picture of Blake's favourite animal, a horse, and slipped the magazine onto Blake's lectern, saying, "don't dob on me".

The classroom remained quiet, the boy got back to his seat without the teacher noticing. Suddenly there was a shriek of delight from Blake as he came across the picture of the horse. His new found friend turned round and whispered fiercely, "I told you not to dob!"

Five years after starting Blake is very much a part of the school.
He is known by everyone and I'm sure the school would say they have benefited from having him there. He has changed attitudes. The creativity needed to make work interesting for Blake has helped the teaching of all children. He has taught everyone in the school that life is not always as it seems.

At long last, after five years of struggling and arguing during reviews, recently there was unanimous agreement from all the professionals that Blake was doing well and was in the right place.

He has had to prove himself over and over again. He will go on having to prove himself when he reaches secondary school. The process will start all over again. It doesn't seem fair. The expectations on Blake are huge – he has to work better than other children at school. His developmental progress is under a spotlight. Socially he has huge expectations placed on him – he has to behave all the time, eat well etc.
I am forcing him to be part of the social world, to conform. Are others forcing themselves to change so our children can be themselves?

I would love to be able to change certain things in this world – prejudice, poverty, violence – but funnily enough, Blake is not on this list. I would not change 'him'. I love 'him' just the way he is, unconditionally, and what I would like for him from others is unconditional respect for who he is.

Anne Williamson

FRIENDSHIPS

The kids in class were writing about friendship. Lots of them included Blake as a friend. This is a new school for Blake so their knowledge of him is only six months old. This made me wonder how kids looked on Blake as a friend.

Sean : "I like Blake a lot. He makes me laugh."

Lauren : "He's OK. I was frightened at first, I thought he would pull my hair."

Laura : "I just like helping him."

David : "Well .... Blake never falls out with me. He's always my friend."

Amy : (When they were at nursery together.) "If Blake's not going to nursery I'm not going."

The kids in school take their lead from the adults. When it is positive and consistent they respond likewise. Blake has difficulty getting up and down from the floor. At the Christmas party I was there if needed. When the children were playing games Blake was only just getting up as everyone else was getting back down. I helped him a couple of times – then the kids took over. Whoever was nearest helped him up.
What this shows is how children accept situations so much more easily. Adults should take note. If children are given the lead, the support and the space, they can teach us a lot by just getting on with it.

Anne Williamson

Dear Annie

Dear Annie

I cried the day I read your postcard out to Kim. Kim has many friends but – with the exception of his sister – they are all much older than him. Apart from Jessie you are the first person his own age who has ever called themselves his friend. As you know he is the same age as you – eleven.

Those three words, "Annie (your friend)", made me think. What is it like to be eleven years old and not have had a friend your own age? My stomach churns at the prospect of this for myself. The truth is I do not know. I cannot imagine. What I can imagine from the deep pit I feel in my stomach is that it must feel awful. Worse than awful.

Kim has been called many things by many people but never "friend" by someone his own age.

I know how quickly friendships change at eleven. I know you may not stay in our lives for long. I hope you do. You have come into our lives like a ray of sunshine and I can feel you melting a frozen part of me. I can feel dreams beginning about possibilities of future friendships Kim might have. With your words you have started the thaw of some deep frozen fear and given me permission to dream.

I have been told Kim does not relate to his peers, he is at his best with adult attention. I have said, "but he loves his sister, Jessie. I know he does. They are very close."

"Aha", they said, "but how do you know he loves his sister?"

"By the way he looks at her", I said.

"But does he go up to her and ask to play?" they said.

"No", I said, "but I know he loves her."

"Oh", they said.

The damage was done. Although I threw away the label they gave to him, that day I took on some of their ideas. I thought that maybe he did not need friends his own age, he has so many other friends.

You have shown me I was wrong.

I was so nervous when you first came round to tea. Would you enjoy being with Kim? Would he live up to your expectations? I worried and wittered to Jessie all week long. You came and we had a good time. You and Kim rolled pizza dough together, you read books together, you watered flowers together. To watch you and Kim be together filled my heart with joy.

Yet I was still anxious. Had you really enjoyed yourself? A few days later you popped in and said you had, it was a good time. You were disappointed Kim was out. You said you would like to come again. As you left you said, "say 'hi' to Kim". More simple words. More sunshine on my frozen block of fear.

Yet still I said to your dad, "next time she comes maybe we can all go swimming." He interrupted me gently, "you don't need to entertain her, you know."

I do know. You only want to be with Kim. To be a friend. To hang around as friends do. I know exactly. Dance in and out of our lives Annie. Continue to teach me, continue to be Kim's friend.

With love from your friend, Pippa.

Pippa Murray

Dear Bethan

Dear Bethan

You have just fallen asleep so I have decided to write you a letter rather than do one of the mundane things I try to do when you're not around.

I hope one day – no, I know one day – you will read this. Unlike all the other children in your class you cannot read or write yet, but I know you will, when you are ready.

You could do now, if you wanted to, but you seem to have much more interesting things to see and do. Life for you seems full of magic.

We seem to timetable our children – should be walking, talking, reading etc. at such and such an age.

When I compare your pride and delight at each small achievement, and the pressure on your elder brother as he prepares for his mock GCSE's I wonder if we have lost something in our education system. Some people will say you cannot compare them, but who knows?!

Just look at you – hunched up in your chair, head back, mouth open, snoring loudly. (We're still waiting for the tonsil and adenoid operation.) At this moment your features, features that label you, are very prominent.

What is sad is that many people will see those features, and only those features, and judge you by them.

I did it only once.

It was the first time I saw you. Your dad and I went to the hospital to meet the social worker. "Here she is", she said, handing me a photograph. You were four months old. I looked at the photo and thought, "what an ugly baby". An hour later I met you. Ugly? You were beautiful!

The flat photograph had not captured you: these bright eyes, crooked smile; young as you were, a personality.

Stories of Inclusion

To me you were perfect – just like other babies. I couldn't understand when people said they could see that you had 'Downs Syndrome'.
I never saw these features all through your babyhood.

I suppose now as you are growing they are more prominent but I only see them when you are asleep, when your personality is closed off. You are such a character.

What is it about you that seems to radiate joy, build bridges? You have such trust in people – the way you walk onto a bus and say to the driver, 'home please', as if he should know where you live.

The way you leave the bus, you wave and say good-bye to each seat so

Bethan Morgan

that we leave a bus full of smiling people.

I often think that if a little bit of that "extra chromosome" was rubbed on all of us there would be no wars, no inequality in the world, just love and acceptance of the uniqueness of each individual.

I have never seen you as needing different "treatment". You have followed in your brother and sister's footsteps. You have gone to local toddler groups, play group, nursery and now local school.

You are a member of the Rainbows, Girls Brigade and a local Sunday School. You are invited out to friends and to lots of birthday parties (how you love them).

You are well known in all the local shops, especially the sweet shop where you shop by yourself. You belong.

As I've said already, your pace is slower and you need a little more help than your peers, but that is your right.

What do I wish for you?

I wish your life to continue in this pattern – you are an important member of the local community.

I hope these loveable little features will not close people's minds – that they will take time to get to know you, and thereby gain a friend for life.

I can only hope your life will be surrounded by love and acceptance, and you will be allowed to use your talents and your love so you can lead a fulfilled life.

Thank you for being my daughter. Thank you for enriching our family life. Thank you for being such a complete person.

All my love, Mummy

Norma Morgan

BETHAN

The very first day Bethan came to live with us I took her down to school to meet Sian, her big sister, who was then six years old. From that day on she has been a regular visitor and it never occurred to us that she should go to any other school.

From the beginning we wanted Bethan to have the same experiences as our two older children – we didn't see why anything should be different. Bethan had a very high profile as a baby. She was well known at the local school – by staff, children and parents – and she was well known in our church community.

She went to toddler group, play group, nursery school, and is now in our local primary school. Inclusion has been a natural process. Before starting school Bethan had years of exploring the building. She knew where everything was – class rooms, toilets, hall. This was great as it was so familiar to her when she went as a pupil.

Because she has always done ordinary things lots of older children at school know her from their days at nursery or play group. She has many friends and is very independent. When I pick her up from school she dashes off to chat with the lollipop lady. She then has to go in to the fruit shop across the road for a chat, and so on until we get home.

Bethan is flourishing, living in this very ordinary way and yet I know how precarious her position is. So far we have been lucky – we have not had to fight for anything. Everything that we have asked for has been given. Sometimes, though, I worry that Bethan is on trial, under a spotlight my older two children do not have to endure.

Norma Morgan

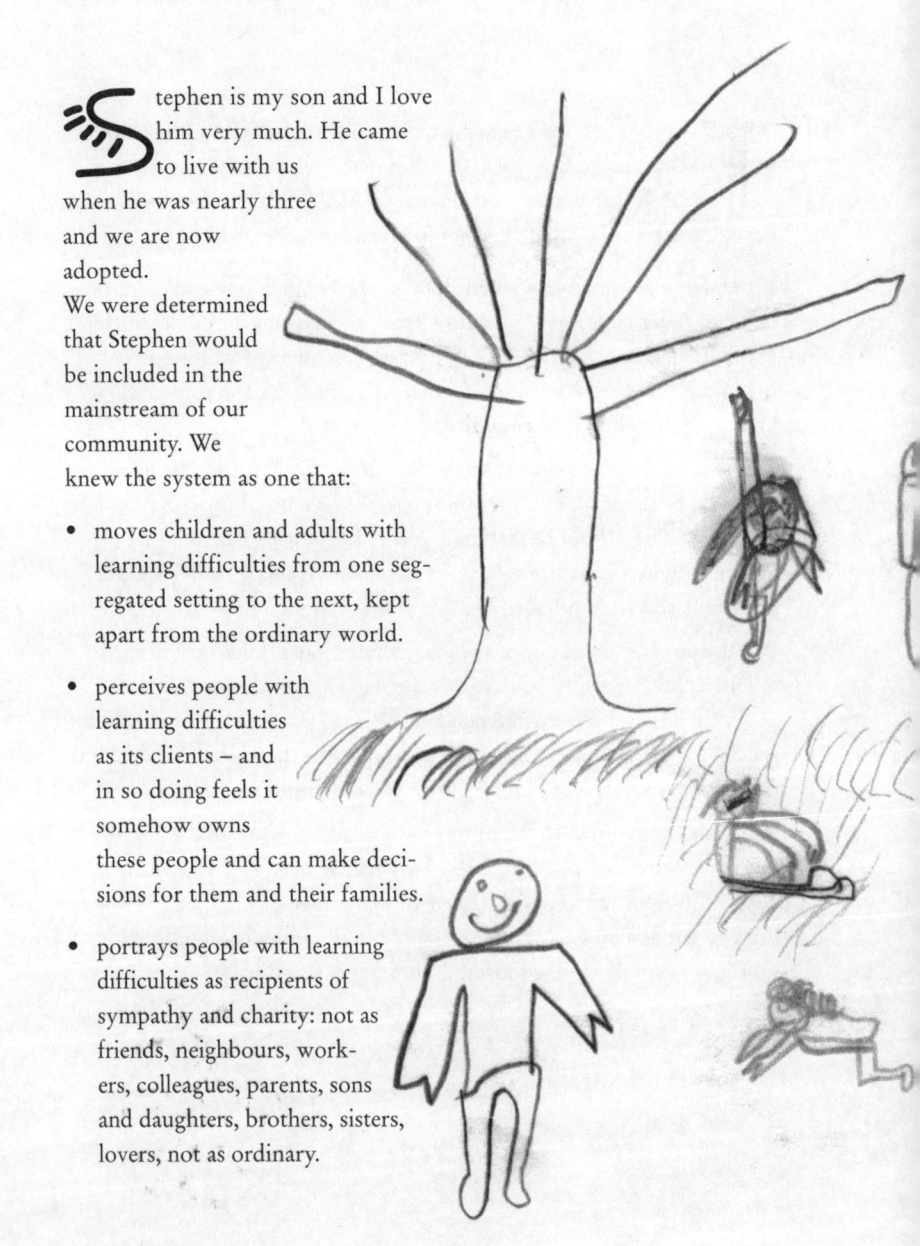

An Ordinary Life

Stephen is my son and I love him very much. He came to live with us when he was nearly three and we are now adopted. We were determined that Stephen would be included in the mainstream of our community. We knew the system as one that:

- moves children and adults with learning difficulties from one segregated setting to the next, kept apart from the ordinary world.

- perceives people with learning difficulties as its clients – and in so doing feels it somehow owns these people and can make decisions for them and their families.

- portrays people with learning difficulties as recipients of sympathy and charity: not as friends, neighbours, workers, colleagues, parents, sons and daughters, brothers, sisters, lovers, not as ordinary.

Stories of Inclusion

And what we want for our child is an ordinary life.

Stephen is my disabled child and I love him very much. I am very proud of him. He is funny and naughty and beautiful and cheeky and wild and loving and kind and stubborn. He brings a lot of joy to people who know him. He approaches life with excitement, trust and a strong desire to participate.

He goes to his local mainstream school, which he attends half days in the mornings. He takes great delight in going down the hill to school each morning, seeing all the other boys and girls making the same journey. He looks out for children he knows. From all our observations he very much enjoys being at school and benefits hugely from his involvement there. It would not occur to him – nor, as far as we can see, to the other children – that he should be anywhere else.

We go and swim and kids who know him from school say hello. They say hello in the street, in the shops, in the pub, in the park.

Wherever we go locally we see children who know him.

In day to day life they know him and he knows them. They are learning about difference and he is included.

Graham Jones
Jill Penman

MY KIND OF COMMUNITY

✓ Sees and welcomes people with all kinds of different gifts
✓ is where we shop
✓ is where we learn
✓ is where the human need is more important than profit
✓ is where we offer support
✓ is where friends are made
✓ is where we can find peace
✓ is where we may worship
✓ is where we share experiences
✓ is where we work
✓ embraces diversity and respects difference
✓ is where we have fun
✓ welcomes a challenge and views it as an opportunity for enrichment
✓ fosters creativity and initiative
✓ is where responsibility is shared
✓ is where spontaneity is encouraged
✓ is where we go to school
✓ links all members of the neighbourhood
✓ is where children play freely
✓ thrives on co-operation
✓ empowers all people

- ✓ is where everyone is heard
- ✓ is where we find support
- ✓ is where we learn to listen
- ✓ is where we learn to look
- ✓ allows us to make mistakes
- ✓ is where we feel safe
- ✓ is where relationships flourish
- ✓ is where there is absence of fear, oppression and tyranny
- ✓ is where conflict can be settled
- ✓ strives for peace, justice and harmony
- ✓ is where we can grow
- ✓ is where we all belong

Stephen Jones

My community is still only partially realised, still partly a dream. But one day my dream will become reality.

Judith Gwynn

Wise and Visionary Teachers

When Kim was first diagnosed as having a "global developmental delay" and "epilepsy" at the age of one, the consultant paediatrician advised me "not to think of the future". The phrase stuck in my mind but until very recently I did not understand why. By telling me not to think about Kim's future that doctor took away my natural instinct to dream for my son – to dream for my son in his own right and on his own. To dream for my son in relation to others, including his own family. The phrase damaged me.

It took me ten years to undo the damage and start dreaming. I now dream big. I listen to my son and I give words to his dreams. I dream positive and possible and I dream positive and impossible – at least in his lifetime.

Kim gave me one of my favourite dreams as we walked through the woods together. We had just spent an hour in a grim "special needs room" in our local school. It felt good to be outside again. The sun was shining, the air brisk and the streams sparkling. Autumn leaves were on the ground. We walked along chatting for a bit. Then we fell into a companionable silence.

I began to imagine the world one hundred years from now. There were more wars all over the world. Rich countries were richer, poor countries were poorer. Rich people were richer, poor people were poorer.

Pollution was greater – many of the trees, plants and wildlife which we have today were extinct. Environmentally, things had most definitely gone downhill. There were more machines, less interaction between people. In this country people in work worked hard and played hard. Unemployed people roamed the streets, homeless and hungry.
The welfare state had collapsed. There were huge health problems for the poor, huge mental health problems for the rich.

Things were continuing to get worse so a learned professor at a leading university decided to do some research into "human happiness".

Stories of Inclusion

This professor had read about the concept but had never experienced it for herself, and knew no-one who had. It would be interesting, she thought, to see what it was, if indeed it still existed at all.

A team of researchers went round the world. They spoke to people in each and every society. No money was spared for this important piece

Matthew and Dad go skiing. They ar HAPPY

Matthew Gwynn

of research. People were curious and desperate. Ten years later all the findings were collated and there was great excitement when it became obvious that some people around the world were happy.

These people were few and far between but they did exist. More research was done as there seemed to be no obvious links between these people. Five years later this was completed and there was more excitement – and disbelief – as the findings were made public.

All the people all over the world who were happy had this one thing in common: all were connected in a true, living, real way to someone with a perceived learning difficulty. To live with someone with a perceived learning difficulty was not enough; there had to be a great relationship and understanding between the two people.

Suddenly people became very interested in disabled people, especially those with learning difficulties. Everyone wanted such a relationship, everyone wanted a chance at being happy. Of course there were not enough people to go round and those with learning difficulties did not all want to move away from their homes. Over the years their status changed. From being at the bottom of the pile they became the most valued people of all societies. Their role as wise and visionary teachers was slowly recognised.

Slowly the world changed.

In the first instance, more individuals became happy, then communities and societies changed as everyone truly listened to their new teachers. Wars were stopped. Environmental damage was reduced, and steps taken to reverse it. People did jobs instead of machines. People began to listen and communicate with their work colleagues and with their neighbours. Material goods were shared between all.

Difference was respected, valued and recognised as necessary. Everyone was seen as having gifts. The gift of leading the way and teaching societies how best to reach their dreams was always acknowledged as coming from the most gifted listeners – those we label as having learning difficulties.

As we walked along I wondered what Kim's role in such a society would be. It did not take long for the answer to pop into my mind. He would be recognised as one of the greatest visionaries of the peace movement. Aged eleven he has never deliberately hurt anyone else, either physically or emotionally. He is a truly gentle person.
People who wanted to learn how to stop wars and feuding would simply spend time with him and he would provide the atmosphere whereby they would find the solution to their problems.

By now we were home again. I looked at Kim in amazement. How many lifetimes will it take to make our dreams possible?

Pippa Murray
With thanks to Kim for giving me the idea through his being

STORIES OF PROFESSIONALS

> We believe that the best people to talk about having a learning difficulty and our rights are those with learning difficulties.

Anya Souza

Inclusive Education Conference, Sheffield, March 1994

severe intractable epilepsy...
unco-operative...
developmental regression...
great strain...
autistic tendencies...
a major problem.

SYLVIA

Sylvia came to me when she was twenty two months old. I was delighted with her and I just wanted to be with her all the time and not think about anything else.

She had been through the assessment process at the child development centre and so was already being seen by numerous people: the paediatrician, physiotherapist, speech therapist, teacher, orthopaedic surgeon, ophthalmic surgeon and on and on and on. I, of course, wanted to do the best for her and help her with the disability. So I kept all the appointments, sometimes three or four a week! I would far rather have gone for walks, lain in bed, played, or have been eating treats in cafes with Sylvia. After two months I was already coming into conflict with people we were seeing. The first thing was about some medication she was on. There was talk about it being increased. I didn't think it was making sense but this was not being questioned at all. So I stopped it, to see what would happen. She became more alert and no more stiff, so after a few weeks I told them and by that time nobody could say how necessary it was. Nobody had asked what I thought.

Then we were going to computer sessions where Sylvia had previously done very well and had enjoyed herself. The teacher, I thought, had started making the sessions into a jumping through hoops exercise rather than having fun – e.g. Sylvia was made to use a complicated set of switches to get results. She was only just two years old at this time. After a few of these sessions Sylvia started screaming when we approached the door so, much against the advice of the teacher, I decided to stop taking her.

After six months I was completely overwhelmed with people telling what I should be doing, with the message that "if you don't do all these things now, when she's young, she won't develop her mobility, communication and so on." I still just wanted to play, have a good time, and try and learn to listen to what Sylvia wanted. I felt that it would all be my fault if Sylvia didn't develop these skills, and yet what

I wanted to do was develop our relationship. It was difficult being in conflict as I had not yet adopted Sylvia and was very conscious of my parenting being assessed.

The adoption committee didn't know much about disability, so were taken in by the 'expertise' on offer. I was lucky enough to have been a health visitor before, and had met various people in the course of my work. One person I had met I didn't know well but remembered that I'd liked what she'd said. She had worked with parents of newly diagnosed disabled children. I rang her to ask if she could come and see me, and she was sensitive enough to come the next day. She gave me the best advice I've ever had: "cancel all your appointments for the next two months, it won't make any difference." I began to relax and see more clearly that my relationship with Sylvia was essential for whatever way she was going to develop. This person then put me in touch with someone else who had adopted a disabled child. That person in turn became very helpful to me.

The next hurdle was nursery. I was given the names of three potentially suitable nurseries. One was attached to a school for 'physically disabled' children, and the other two were social services nurseries taking twenty percent of 'special needs' children. I went to see all three and decided I liked one of the social services ones. Immediately the special needs teacher said she thought that would be wrong as the one attached to the school for 'physically disabled' children would have all the specialist input that Sylvia needed. Again I felt very undermined: I had still only had Sylvia for eight months; the adoption hadn't yet gone through and I felt insecure. So although I put off nursery attendance for another year, I was again, because of my uncertainty, persuaded against my better judgement that maybe 'they' were right about the specialist input. Maybe I just didn't know.

When Sylvia did eventually go to nursery she was nearly four. I decided three mornings a week was the right amount of time; I'd see how she settled. Again I was severely criticised by both the nursery and the educational psychologist, who thought she should be going full time (a lot of two and three year olds are going five full days). The fact that Sylvia was completely exhausted by half past eleven in the morning,

Stories of Professionals

and fell asleep the minute we got into the car, appeared to mean nothing to them. I was just over protective. They also thought I shouldn't bring her to nursery; she should go on the transport (again, a lot of two and three year olds spend up to one and a half hours each end of the day, going to and from nursery). I tried to go on the bus with Sylvia one week (which was very much against the rules) and Sylvia just sat there, rigid with fear, not looking anywhere. Of course I decided I was going to carry on taking her to nursery myself, which I was quite happy to do anyway. What was said about that reduced me to tears but luckily I didn't budge.

When I tried to raise the fact that being adopted might mean it would take longer for her to trust people and settle in, this was not responded to at all. Disabled children aren't supposed to have feelings!

So the conflict continued: she needed a nursery, she needed other children, but the way I was made to feel about what I thought was completely undermining. Gradually Sylvia relaxed, and by the end of the first year she was staying for lunch, then for three full days a week, but never full time.

I also found review meetings a nightmare. I felt I was listening to people talk about somebody other than the child I lived with. After the first review at the child development centre I went home and cried for four days. I then asked the physiotherapist if I could have the report that parents are given at the first full assessment for diagnosis (this had been done when Sylvia was ten months, before she was in care). I was told I couldn't have it and anyway there was no point because I wouldn't understand it. I did eventually get it, but again it was hard work and very undermining of my trying to build a picture of what was going on.

The same tone went on at nursery; at one review meeting the speech therapist asked if the staff could wait for Sylvia to respond to questions (she would eventually nod or turn away). The answer was that they didn't have time for such things – this in the place I'd been persuaded to send Sylvia, because of its specialist input! Then, when she was five and a half, they decided they didn't want her at that school anyway.

It had become evident to me by the time Sylvia was four years old that her main difficulty was that of communication. I was confused and wondered if this was a withdrawal as much as a neurological problem. Both the teacher and the psychologist from the child development centre, after going through the usual developmental assessment routine, said they had thought that Sylvia, at two years old, had severe physical difficulties but no learning difficulties. Now, though, they realised they had been wrong as it was quite clear she did indeed have severe learning difficulties. Then without further discussion they walked out of my house, leaving me to piece it all together. After a few weeks, having talked to the speech therapist at school (with whom I got on very well), the psychologist came back and admitted she didn't know what was going on with Sylvia. But by that time I had lost all trust in anyone at the child development centre.

When nursery decided that Sylvia shouldn't go on to its attached school I decided to look at other schools. After seeing about six I decided on one where the atmosphere seemed good and Sylvia seemed very welcome. So we moved in order that she could attend. After five or six weeks I was collared by the teacher, one afternoon when leaving with Sylvia, and told the school just couldn't cope with children like her. Sylvia heard this and the next day she bit one of the other children. She had made clear her feelings about not being welcome.

I had two good friends with children in the same class as Sylvia. They spoke up for Sylvia and me over the next year and, having looked at more schools, I decided I wouldn't move her again. She and I are now very welcome in this school but it has made me ask lots of questions about both health and educational services for all disabled children.

When I think back to that first six months after Sylvia came to me it is clear that the essential process of bonding happened in spite of the specialist input I was getting. It seems to me that everything should be geared to helping the child feel loved as she is, however insecure, unhappy, frightened; however stiff, however little she can do: geared to helping the new parent love this child as she is now, not how she might be in the future.

It is well known that children must feel wanted for how they are before they can flourish and change, and I'm sure everyone involved with Sylvia and me would have agreed. So why did it feel such a struggle? Much of my story is the same for all parents of disabled children. We do need help but our children, rather than having 'special' needs, have additional needs to the needs all children have. And all children have emotional needs.

Over the past six years nobody in the education field has acknowledged Sylvia's losses and hurts. At the beginning (when she was only two years old and people were pushing her to perform) I tried to say that I felt she needed space to do just what she wanted, even if that was nothing, but no one heard. Again, when going to nursery and fearful of the change, I tried to explain that it seemed quite reasonable to be frightened of change given her early life history. But they looked at me as if I were mad. Then when we moved and Sylvia started school she wouldn't do anything or make eye contact – she just looked away. Nobody appreciated that she was probably desperately frightened, and needed welcoming.

Early interventionist help is of course very well meant, and parents of disabled children do need help. What happens, I think, is that the help is based on 'improving' the child for the benefit of the world or society she/he lives in, not for the child to get more out of life. That is, the help is based on the needs of a world with aggressive attitudes to disability rather than on the need of the child to make relationships, communicate, play, give and learn about the world. The professionals are in the difficult position of being the agents of this need the world has for a performing or 'independent' child.

The distress a parent feels when her child is diagnosed as disabled, or when her child is not developing as expected, is the distress of having to meet head on the 'ableism' that the culture has faced her with.
For some this is so huge that they abandon their relationship with the child. It seems to me that most parents don't need help to love their child. They need physical and financial help, and help to look at what their culture has made them feel about disabled people. The professional helper/educator has most probably not fallen in love with a disabled child and so has not had to face her own 'ableism'. The

professional helper probably won't be listening to the child. There are notable exceptions, but this is what most parents are having to deal with. The professional helper will be emphasising the expectations of the world and will be aiming to 'help' the child not to fail in those expectations. This is most likely an impossible task.

Parents and children in this position do need help but it must come from outside this oppressive viewpoint. The help must come from being completely child-centred, which must include the parent as well. Taking time, listening, playing, laughing, appreciating; this is what is so hard to come by. The alternative to the usual pressure is to be abandoned by the system and get nothing at all – which of course isn't right either.

I felt lucky. Sylvia has always been a very attractive child, easy to take out and about, so the negative input from some of the professionals was usually balanced out by people in shops and elsewhere talking to her, laughing with her and enjoying her. I would like to say here that some people we are seeing on a professional basis really stood out as saving the day, so there are notable exceptions to what I'm saying. But these people are also struggling against the system.

When I have felt vulnerable at those times when somebody has been very negative about Sylvia's lack of progress, I have felt I could hardly look at her or feel good about her at all; I have thought that all the good things I felt must have been fantasies or wrong; that I should never have had her because she would have progressed much better with another family. On the other hand if I felt vulnerable and somebody just said how beautiful Sylvia was, or what a great sense of humour she had, and how nice it was when she was so pleased to see them again, I immediately felt I was doing a good job, however tiring it might be. Then I felt good about myself and our relationship. What a tightrope we all walk!

I have had to adjust to the fact that so far Sylvia has developed very differently from what was predicted when I first had her. This has been difficult but it has also been exciting, and has changed the way I see things. I have made friends with other parents of disabled children, and with them I can share a lot of the thoughts and feelings I have expressed here. I have also made other friends who have been real allies in the bad times.

Adoption can be a precarious process: when a child has more difficulties than expected the relationship goes through traumas and needs nurturing and help. This help needs to come from somebody in an adoption department or post adoption service whose prime responsibility is to nurture that relationship. Above all, I needed Sylvia to be welcomed and wanted wherever and whoever she was. We didn't often get that; particularly not in the education and health world.

Having a child changes your life. Adopting a child brings with it more issues which bring further changes. Disability brings even more change. It's not surprising then that we need appreciation and concrete help at times.

So to be able to nurture a relationship with an adoptive parent and a disabled child, professionals must feel comfortable and enjoy the child as he or she is now. They must be able to express that enjoyment to the parent, able to see what the child is giving to her environment. This, I think, is the most effective remedy for the oppression.

Caroline MacKeith

MY CHILD

The following descriptions of Kim were taken from professional reports and comments on the one hand; descriptions by family and friends on the other.

✍ He shows a moderate developmental delay at two years eight months, with skills falling a little further behind due to a developmental plateau.

☀ Kim's a toddler with a great laugh and a lot of energy.

✍ He is showing a marked developmental regression.

☀ Kim tries so hard all the time. He never gives up.

✍ He has severe intractable epilepsy and will need to be placed in a special school with a special care unit.

☀ Kim is an ordinary lad who needs to do ordinary things with all other children his own age.

✍ He is very passive.

☀ Kim is so easy to be with.

✍ He has autistic tendencies.

☀ Kim communicates so beautifully.

✍ He is often uncooperative.

☀ Kim is easy going.

Stories of Professionals

- ✎ He can't behave like that. He simply has to stop!
- ☀ I love it when he gets excited. His enthusiasm is so infectious.

- ✎ He needs respite care.
- ☀ Kim needs baby-sitters and friends.

- ✎ He has frequent seizures. These constitute a major problem.
- ☀ Kim has frequent seizures. They are a part of him.

- ✎ He has complex communication difficulties.
- ☀ Being with Kim allows me to be myself – to get away from all peer pressures, and pressures of the world.

- ✎ He has severe learning difficulties.
- ☀ Kim teaches me more than I can ever teach him. He is the best teacher I've ever had.

- ✎ He has co-ordination difficulties. He does not have full mobility.
- ☀ I love the way Kim moves. When he is very poorly and lifts his arm so slowly I wonder at the grace of his movement.

- ✎ Due to his severe epilepsy he has variable function.
- ☀ Sometimes Kim is energetic, sometimes he's tired.

- ✎ Due to his problems the family will experience great strain over the summer holidays.
- ☀ No professionals for six weeks. Hooray!

Pippa Murray

Becoming Different

My partner and I wanted to adopt and we wanted to adopt a disabled child. This was no act of charity. We had both had some very enjoyable relationships with disabled children we had met. It was our view, confirmed by our experience four years on, that to include a disabled child in our family would bring us great joy. Our son is a delight to us and we are very proud of him.

From making this decision I, for the first time in my experience, ceased to be 'ordinary' and came to be perceived in a negative way, as 'different'. I had not changed but was being treated differently. As a non-disabled white man I had not experienced exclusion or discrimination – nor had I expected to. Life, and the way I experience it, has changed.

The exclusion my son experiences and, because we love and support him, our whole family by association shares in, has given me a far greater understanding of the various ways exclusion functions.
For that knowledge I am grateful; it has made me a wiser person. That said, I wanted to deny what was happening to us. I feared that engaging with the reality of exclusion would damage us more than keeping it at arm's length. My partner knew better – it is not possible to fend off –and she has actively sought out support networks. As a man, I have found it hard to accept the need for support – yet I know it is not possible to survive without it.

One of the most obvious ways in which life has changed has been the contact we are obliged to have with a range of 'professionals'. I feel it necessary to say I am not anti-professional: we have encountered good professionals, and when this process began I myself was on a Social Work course, training to be a Probation Officer.
Overall, though, my son and my family's treatment by professionals leaves me angry and saddened.
Professionals have come into my home, depressed and miserable, telling

me what a hard day they have had. They have been so late for appointments we have decided they were not coming – only to have them arrive saying how busy they are. When a professional arrives late, saying how busy they are, they say by implication that what they do is more important than what we do. They have been so late for appointments we have decided they were not coming – and we were right, they didn't turn up at all. In meetings they have made sweeping statements based on the briefest actual contact with my son. If we disagree with professionals in meetings they get angry and try not to show it (they fail!). If we disagree, we don't appreciate the efforts they are making; the difficulties they face. We underestimate our son's abilities; overestimate our son's abilities, we don't understand how difficult he can be; don't know what schools are for – and so on and on and on.

When we telephoned the relevant Social Work team for some general information, no social worker was available. Some weeks later we received a letter saying no social worker could be 'allocated' to us at this stage unless our 'situation deteriorated'. But we did not want a social worker allocated, nor was our 'situation' in any crisis. We just wanted some information. Some months later a social worker phoned to say he had been allocated our case. When could he come round, and who in the family should he meet first? We had only asked for some information, honest!

We were asked why we wanted to adopt a disabled child, which was a legitimate question. But the conversation that followed served only to display the social worker's prejudice and ignorance: "some of them eat grass, you know".

The difficulty in talking with most of the professionals we have encountered, about disability, our son's support needs and our own support needs is that we are talking about totally different things. The professional's view of disability is based in the myth of 'normality', the myth against which any 'difference' is measured and found wanting, found to be 'abnormal'. This is not, and never can be, the basis on which a professional can empower a 'service user' and provide support and services of real benefit. Such attitudes simply perpetuate the exclusion.

In time the exclusion of disabled people will be understood for what it is – a systematic oppression that is morally unacceptable, the perpetuation of which is to the detriment of everyone in our diverse society.

There was a television programme recently, called Visions of Hell. My vision of hell is the myth of normality being real: – everyone the same; no spark, no imagination, no difference ...NO THANKS.

Graham Jones

TO BE CONTINUED

Our situation today is that we have two sons aged six and a half and four. They both attend the same school. It isn't a special school and it hasn't got an integrated resource. It's an ordinary Nursery/Infant/Junior (N/I/J) school in Heeley Ward.
The elder boy is in Y2, the younger in nursery.
Both have friends asking to come to our house and go on outings with us; both get invited to parties and to friends' houses to play. In fact the situation is just what we would have expected and wanted, a little over three years ago when our elder son was starting at the nursery, and the younger was a child of eleven months who seemed to be doing alright. We took it for granted that one brother would follow the other.

The difference between then and now, and what we never imagined, is that the younger one has a statement of Special Educational Needs (SEN) and needs full time support to go to our local school.
For twelve months of his life we lost any idea of our younger son having such an ordinary experience in his ordinary neighbourhood school. We were told that he was brain damaged, epileptic, has severe learning difficulties. We had no notion of him having any rights.
And – what I think is a common experience for parents when they first receive such a diagnosis for their child – everyone knew more about him than we did.

Someone knew more about his brain than we did; someone else knew more about his speech, his hearing, the way he walked. We easily fell into believing that someone else knew better about the sort of lifestyle he should have, the sort of friends he needed, the sort of school he should go to. So when a Health Visitor told us to put his name down for a Day Nursery we did just that. When an Under Fives Support Teacher told us to put his name down for a Special School Nursery we did that as well!

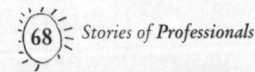

We had no idea at the time that finances were playing a part in the options we were being given. No one told us that a mainstream school with a support worker was an option on the same level as the choices of special school or an integrated resource. I have since asked someone in education: why aren't parents told about that option? I was told they couldn't encourage parents to try for mainstream schools for their disabled children because the struggle involved in getting enough support for a place is too much to expect parents to go through. I personally think that's an indictment on the services of this city if people working directly with parents are unable to tell us what our entitlement is, on the grounds it's too difficult to get it!

We did manage to get back to a position of giving our son the ordinary experience of an ordinary school. Several things helped. First we met parents whose children had a statement of SEN, and attended local schools with support from Child Care Assistants (CCAs) – children with a wide range of diagnoses and abilities. It became a practical possibility for our son to have that chance too.

Secondly, we found out that he had rights. He was entitled to go, with appropriate support, to the school his parents chose – and the limitations to that right were laid down in law. SNAG, a local parents group, was very helpful to us and so were national parents' organisations such as Network 81, in that we could check out with them what our son's entitlement actually was, and we could check out the worth of other things we were told.

We were told the usual things: "If he needs one to one support he'll have to go to a special school." "Whatever he needs, you'll only be offered point two of a CCA." "He won't cope in an ordinary environment, the other kids will bully him."

It's frightening to think what would have happened if we'd believed all those things. We would have had a very different family life to the one we have today. Fortunately, we could check it all out and establish what was just someone's opinion – or local policy within the Education Department – and what was actually relevant in affecting his rights as a disabled child.

Something else that was positive for us at this time was that we were having a lot of good experiences. We were still going to the local toddler group that we had always gone to, where everyone had known our son all his life. The fact that he had been diagnosed as having severe learning difficulties didn't make him any different from the way he'd been before. It just helped to explain why he wasn't learning skills at the same rate as the others. He still belonged as part of the group.

A Portage worker was coming to the house once a week, setting tasks for us to work with our son at home. This introduced us to the idea of partnership between parents and professionals, and we realised that as well as receiving all the advice, we could contribute ideas about his learning. We started to get back some confidence and pride in being his parents.

A particularly good thing was that the Pre-School Playgroups Association (PPA) scheme came to our notice for supporting children with special needs on a one to one basis with their own support worker in an ordinary play group. When our son was two and three quarters he started on the scheme and went to play group for one morning a week. He liked it and, most important for us, we realised that he could manage without us and that with the right person giving appropriate support he could manage in a mainstream environment.

At this stage we committed ourselves to keeping our son in mainstream living with its ordinary experiences.

When he was nearly three and had been on the waiting list for eleven months, he was offered a place at the assessment nursery in the special school. We turned it down and took him off the list. Shortly after his third birthday the statementing procedure began and, when asked for the parents' opinion, we outlined our reasons for wanting him to go to his local nursery and then school.

I'll highlight a couple of things that I think have made it work well so far. We had a positive attitude from all the professionals in the education field. They knew we were committed to sending our son to his local school and no one tried to persuade us that a special school would provide a better quality of education for him. After a couple of meetings with the LEA at the draft stage, the final statement we were given identified his needs accurately. It says he needs to be consistently involved with ordinary children in his neighbourhood, that he needs good role models and the opportunity to make friends with them, and so on. No one put obstacles in his way. What they did do, was to be honest about the question of resources. They told us how difficult it would be to get funding for a support worker. We had a letter from the LEA at one stage, saying there was no money earmarked for under fives with SEN to be supported in a local nursery school, and that any money used to fund mainstream support for under fives was being taken out of the budget meant to give mainstream support to school age children. If we wanted to send our son outside his local community to a special school or to a resource, money could be found quite easily – including for transport! - but it was very difficult getting it for CCA support in the school at the top of the road.

None of this was great news of course, but it was good for us to be told. We could focus on where the difficulty is – resources. Everyone, including the LEA, supported the principle that our son deserved the choice of going to his local school. The struggle was all about resources. It was the same with the local school. When we told the Head that we wanted him in that school, it was a matter of course: he lived in the catchment area, had a brother already in the school; he should have the same opportunity to go there as the next child. The anxiety immediately was about resources. For it to work there had to be funding for proper support.

I'm sure it is obvious why it is working well for us now. He has fifteen hours a week support, with a CCA attached to the class as his support worker all the time he is there. So he is able to go to nursery every morning like all the other children. As well as the one to one help with his learning, it allows him to be included in the class. I could give lots of examples. When they go to the TV room he holds hands with another child to cross the yard – the support worker watching to prevent danger. At play time he goes out with a group of kids – the support worker there to help them take turns, ensure safety, help him build up relationships.

When he needs help putting on his coat or a painting apron, or at the toilet, another four year old is encouraged to do it. The support worker is there to reinforce it so the kids learn that he's one of them, whom they just have to help along a bit. Because he has appropriate support for his needs, he's not seen as a disruption to the class and he's not taking more than his fair share of attention from the general staff ratio.

Most other parents are glad he's there and that their children are growing up learning about disability without the fear and ignorance our generation had. When we meet kids in the street they just say, "It's so and so – he's in my class". It's no big deal to them.

The result for our family of course is great. As I said at the beginning, both our boys have friends, both are well known to other families in the community, both have all the advantages of an ordinary life.

I think it is a positive picture. So long as there is adequate support our son will be able to enjoy education at his local school. But in September, when he moves into the reception class, all his friends will have the right to go for five days a week and the question for us is, will there be the resources to give enough support for him to go for five days? Because to send him to school with inadequate support would be to risk the destruction of all the good practice I've described.

We are wondering if our choice is going to be between part time education on the one hand; on the other, segregating him from his circle of friends in the community, in a special school or integrated resource in another area of the city. If that's the choice I don't think it squares very well with the policy of equal opportunities that Sheffield is so proud of. I think something's wrong with the way money is allocated for special needs education – and I think we all ought to be working together to get it changed.

Paul & Agnes Jenkinson

AT WHAT COST TO OUR CHILDREN?

Segregation is unthinkable – but at present mainstream schools do not value our children. it is not an easy choice.
We've been at this school – our local school – for two years now, and for two years we've been trying to explain it is the school that must change and not the child. It seems the school cannot understand.

It is explained to us again and again what schools are like – as if we didn't know – that if schools are like this then the child is the problem. So are we, of course, because we can't or won't accept this.

It is explained to us that children must be able to sit still, be quiet, concentrate, not disrupt other children: to 'progress' in order to move on with their peers.

"He can't sit still", I explain. "I've said this all along. You can't expect him to. He needs support with this. That is how he is."

I try to imagine what it must be like to be in his place, to be perceived and treated as he is. It fills me with pain, with anger, with frustration and with despair.

It makes me want to keep him completely out of the system as it is today.

And it makes me dream of a system that might be, of schools that might be, where all children belong by right and are celebrated.

So we will carry on trying to explain – it is the schools that must change and not the children.

Name withheld

HOSPITALITY

Hospitals, I hate them. I've been going to hospitals since I was born so I have a lot of experience of hospitality.

They do things to me which are not always necessary, like checking my heart beat going the same 'boom', 'boom', 'boom'.

Checking how much fat I've got – and that's none, by the way!

Once they took a piece out of my back, which I think was for their benefit, not mine.

The worst is that I have to go up and down, round and round the hospital for other doctors to see another part of my body.

When I go in for consultation there are students there, and my mum has to mention it to the doctor because they never ask my mum or me if it is all right. It makes me feel like a freak with them all staring at me.

I would like to be seen by just the one person. I would like them to ask me if they can do things to me and why they have to do it. I want to be seen as a person, not pieces of junk.

My mum wants that too.

Freddy Morrison

Dear Doctor

Dear Doctor

I came to see you today bringing you my most precious gift. My son. So perfect just the way he is. So wonderful, so loving, so giving, so patient, so peaceful, so undemanding, so good at allowing his friends and family to be just the way they want to be.

You did not see him that way. "I have a few ideas for you to think about", you said. "We might be able to stop this developmental regression. We might be able to stop some of the damage that happens to him through his seizures."

To me "this developmental regression" is part of him. I love every part of him. He would not be the son I know and love if the "developmental regression" were not there. Can you hear me doctor? Can you hear me with your heart?

I say again: I love my son just as he is. I want the world to accept him just as he is. That is the biggest dream I have for my son – to be allowed to be.

Do I ask for the moon, the sun or the stars? Is this so much to ask, too much to dream? It seems so.

You asked me to think about having his brain chopped in two – to try and stop the damage, the physical injuries, the developmental regression. There would of course be risks to this procedure, you said. It may or may not work. It may cause more damage, but as his learning difficulties are already so great we might not notice the further damage too much. I should think about it.

Would you chop your brain in two? No, don't tell me it's different for you. Don't tell me you don't "suffer" from his seizures, his learning difficulties. I ask you again – would you chop your brain in two?

I felt deep pain, damage and scarring as I left your office with my son, my perfect gift to the world. Time will lessen the pain. The scars you made on me today will fade but they will never go away.

I will not allow my son to be mutilated in this way. I will cry and hurt for a bit and then I shall begin to dream again. Dream that my son is allowed to be.

Name withheld

LET OUR CHILDREN BE

As this collection developed, a list of themes emerged – being, difference, humanity, labels, power, rights, love, hope, courage, journeying, dreaming, belonging. Each of these themes is woven throughout the collection as a whole. As a list they prompted the following piece, which we have written for people who work with our families in particular.

- ✓ Please allow our children to be. To be just as they are.
  Being is essential, it is about identity, about existence.
  Being is the essence of ourselves.
  Our children have the right to be.

- ✓ Please welcome difference. Difference teaches us about ourselves and each other.
  Do not allow your fear of our children to spoil the opportunities they offer and the gifts they bring.

- ✓ Please acknowledge our children's humanity. Do not treat them as less than human.

- ✓ Please try to accept that our children are ordinary children.
  We are not interested in your labels for them.

- ✓ Please try to accept that we do what we believe is best for our children. This is no different from the majority of parents.
  When we do not share your perceptions of our children, understand that we recognise the labels you give to us, also.

- ✓ Please recognise your power. Think very carefully about the messages you give when you talk to us about our children and their futures.

- ✓ Please recognise that we are tired of our children being treated as the property of professionals.
  Do not tell us to be patient. Our children are children now.

If their time is wasted they do not get it back. Understand our anger if you tell us you know what is best for them.

✓ Please understand that we love our children very much.
  This may be difficult for you, since you perceive them as defective.

✓ Please recognise we are on a journey.
  We are travelling towards a point in the future where all children are of equal value.

✓ Please understand that we are absolutely serious when we talk about the need for change.
  We will not accept present discrimination.
  When we say all children must be included, we mean all children. All does mean all.

Pippa Murray
Jill Penman

> Let us create together a powerful enchantment.
> Let inclusion be in my lifetime.

Judith Snow

Enchantment for Inclusion, in **Learning Together Magazine***, Issue 4, March 1993*

Matthew Cooks Mar-
to buy Sausages. We
and Sparklers and Ma
Sausages and a Camp

Mallows while I go
Having Fireworks
Mallows and
tonight.

by
Simon
Gwynn

matthew

Lovely Mallows

MY BROTHER AND ME

I am five years old and look a lot like my father.
I am three years old and look a bit like my mum.

When I was two and a half, mum wanted me to go to play group for one morning per week. She had my little brother to look after as well. I wanted to stay with them. I said "no" to play group. "Not till I'm a bigger boy."

> *When I was not even two, mum was told that I ought to go to a day nursery for two full days a week. They told her to join a daytime course to take her mind off me for a while. I said nothing. I had no speech.*

I call her mum. My friends at school and their mums and dads, my friends on our street and at Boys Brigade and Sunday School all know her as Joe's mummy.

> *I say mama – but to quite a few different things. My health visitor and social worker, my therapists and G.P. all see her as Sam's carer.*

I know about families. We've done them at school. There are four of us in my family: mum and dad, my brother and me.

> *Mum and dad were offered help to look after me at home. It involved me going away from home to somewhere else at the weekend. It would give my mum and dad and brother some time together as a family.*

*Stories of **Brothers & Sisters***

> Brekfst Time at ore house
>
> At Breakfast this morning I tuck 2 of Sam's slise of Tose bicrse he tuck 1 of mine and mine are bigger than his so weev got the same amort still
>
> Joe

Joe Jenkinson

I have a baby sitter so that mum and dad can have a night out on their own.

> *I have a respite carer because mum and dad need a rest from the burden of looking after me.*

I am sturdy and strong. I can duck and weave and push and shove. They say I have the makings of a rugby prop forward.

> *I am always running around people's feet and bumping into people. I'm big for my age so I'm difficult to handle. Kids like me are often strong as well. It's another problem with us.*

I am very lively and into everything. I'm always busy, keeping myself amused until a grown up spoils my fun!

> *I can't settle. I have poor concentration. I do not cooperate with adult intervention in my play.*

Stories of Brothers & Sisters

I am exceptionally friendly and outgoing. I'll go to anybody and am never any trouble if mum leaves me with someone else.

> *My social awareness is poorly developed. I do not behave appropriately and am not wary of strangers.*

I don't have a label of my own. My family is labelled so I get a fair share. Whether my brother can go to school, whether my friends get to know my brother in the playground – all this has implications for me.

> *I have many labels. I am epileptic, hyperactive, developmentally delayed with severe learning difficulties. I have so many labels you can hardly see me for them.*

My name is Joe. When I grow up I want to drive a spaceship.
> *My name is Sam. When I grow up…*

Agnes Jenkinson

Dear Bethan

Dear Bethan

You came into my life when I was six years old. I had always wanted a little sister. At the time I didn't know what was wrong with you.

I fell in love with you immediately. When you were home I just wanted to hold you. I wanted to show you to everyone. I was so proud.

Even though you aren't my sister by birth you might as well be. I love you so much. No matter what I do you always forgive me.

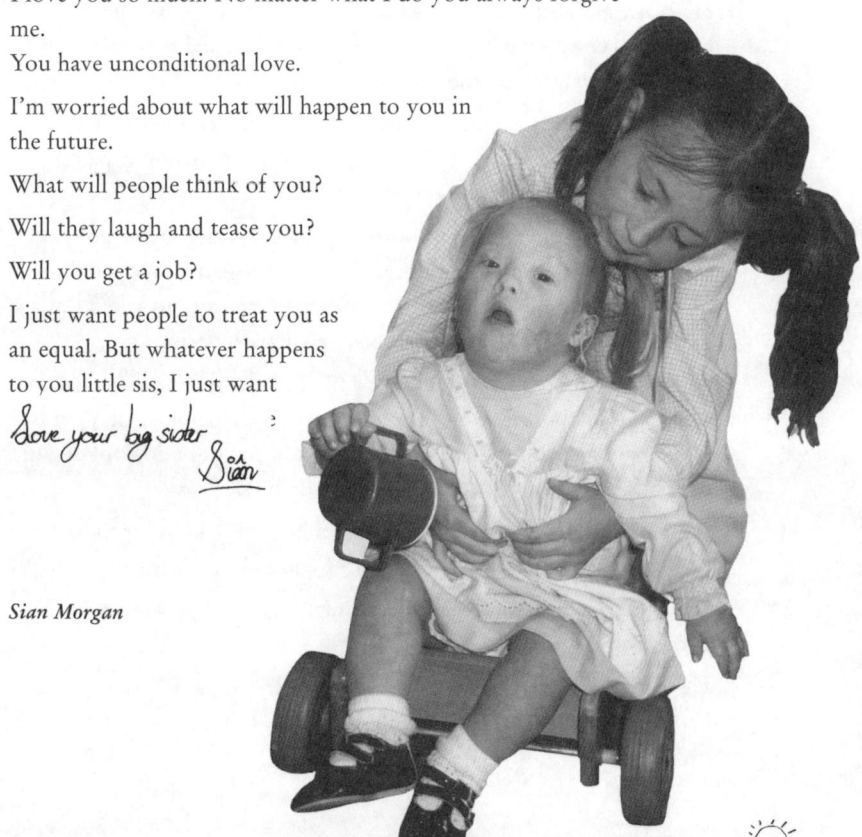

You have unconditional love.

I'm worried about what will happen to you in the future.

What will people think of you?

Will they laugh and tease you?

Will you get a job?

I just want people to treat you as an equal. But whatever happens to you little sis, I just want

Love your big sister
Sian

Sian Morgan

FOR LILY

I sit here and look at you Lily – lying fast asleep – remarkable, beautiful, confident baby child.
I feel such awe and I feel so fortunate.

I sit here and look at you and I'm wondering what life has in store for you.

What will it be like for you being our daughter?

What will life be like for you being Stephen's sister?

You will get many gifts from him – he has such a lot to teach us about.

He is already deeply concerned for your well-being – last night he heard you crying while I was putting him to bed and he was worried about you, wanting to know why you were upset.

He is putting toys in front of you – the ones he knows you like – to amuse you and is regularly checking out how you're doing, patting you on the head, asking you, "Y'all right 'ily?"

He is feeding you at every opportunity, ever so carefully waiting for you to open your mouth to put the spoon in – giving you your bottle of juice to have a drink, giving you his crisps and sweets when I'm not looking, taking his role of looking after you very seriously.

He's letting you sit on his tummy while he's lying on the floor encouraging you to bounce up and down to play 'horsey horsey don't you stop' – both of you joining in the singing as you both do, looking into each other's eyes, both laughing with delight.

When we go to collect him from school he is very keen for the other boys and girls to see you and he kisses you publicly, proudly.

When he wakes in the middle of the night his first question is invariably, "Baby?"

He is very pleased that you have come to live with us – that you are his baby.

Yes, he loves you Lily – he's told me so.

But I have to warn you Lily that you will be told other things too.

You will be told that your brother "has limited intellectual ability", that "he is showing global developmental delay", that "he has intrinsic learning difficulties", that "he is very retarded".

You will be told that his relationships with other people are not as significant to him as your relationships are to you, that he's not capable of feeling things like you are capable of feeling them.

You will be told that you should be concerned about the way your brother is – that it's a problem to have differences.

You will be told that he should be assessed and investigated and provided with special help and therapy – that he should be sent to special other places because he is difficult to include in the places you go to.

You will be told much more.

I have to tell you about all this Lily because it will be so.

Stephen went to play with friends this morning and wanted to take you with him. He didn't agree that you were too small – he's probably right.

I sit here and look at you Lily – lying fast asleep – remarkable, beautiful, confident baby child.

I wonder what you are dreaming about.

I wonder what your dreams will be.

Jill Penman

LILY

Lily is one of my best friends. Lily is one. I am thirteen. That doesn't matter! Sometimes me and Lily go to the park.

We do all sorts of things.
Sometimes I take Lily to see the ducks.
Sometimes Lily takes me to go and see trees.
Sometimes Lily helps me push the buggy.
Sometimes Lily tries to swim with the ducks.
Sometimes we feed the ducks.
Sometimes I sing to Lily.
Sometimes Lily sings with me.
Sometimes me and Lily dance together.
But sometimes we just sit and talk about trees and ducks, or anything that takes our fancy.

Lily is a real friend even if I did not see her for thirty years I would still think of her every day and count her as one of my very special friends.

I used to think a one year old could never be friends with a thirteen years old but now I know that age doesn't matter!

When I was little I was teased about my little brother being seen as 'different'. I had no friends that could understand the pain it gave me as everyone thought I was too little to understand. But I still remember. And if it ever happens to Lily, I will always be there for her.

Jessie Murray

DINNER

I took Kim for dinner today like I do every Tuesday.
Kim was not very well today so Kim went in his wheelchair.

Problems

1. We could not get out of school because of the step down to the courtyard.

2. When we finally got down the steps we couldn't get up to the dinner room.

3. When we got up the step into the dinner room we could not get past the tables!

NO GOOD

4. Nowhere to have dinner.

5. We had to have dinner outside. (It was November.)

6. When we got back into school we had to go upstairs. I carried Kim. My friend carried the wheelchair.

7. Getting back to Kim's form room I had to push Kim through big heavy fire doors and open the doors. At the same time two people walked past. No one HELPED.

Solution

I now get my friends to help me. I find the table, my friends get
our dinner and we sit down and have jokes and tell stories
and Kim's favourite subject to talk about is noses!!!

Jessie Murray

The Future is Assured

I look at you in awe, Jess, and wonder at the privilege I have in being your mother.

I had little idea, fourteen years ago, of the journey we would travel together, of the places you would take me, of the lessons you would teach me. Like many new inexperienced parents I assumed it was me who would be teaching you, me who would be guiding you through life. Over the years we have spent together you have taught me otherwise. It has been you who has taught me such big important lessons. You have taught me how to love unconditionally. You have taught me it is my role as your parent to enable you to be who you are. You have taught me the meaning of allowing my close family and friends to be. To be themselves. You have taught me to stop trying to change people so that they fit in with my picture of the world.

I remember an evening when you were seven and Kim was five. He had just gone to a segregated school and seemed to be coming home with new labels around him every night. Having put Kim to bed I sat on the stairs, surrounded by books and pamphlets, and cried. You knew why I was crying. You came to me and hugged me, saying "Mum, it's all right. It doesn't matter what other people think or say. To us Kim is just Kim and we love him just as he is."

The truth is that you loved him just as he is. I had to learn to love him just as he is. Don't mistake me. I have always loved him but in the early years of diagnosis and labelling I had to fight my way towards the understanding that has grown so quickly and naturally in you. For several years I worked with Kim on intensive programmes which were meant to make him more like other, "ordinary" children. There were many benefits to these programmes but my reason for doing them was wrong. Instinctively you seemed to know that. You never liked the programmes or felt at ease with them. Kim felt the same and so we stopped them. I still did not quite understand. Over the years I learned to stand back and look at Kim through your eyes. You allow him to be. He is your brother, no one special,

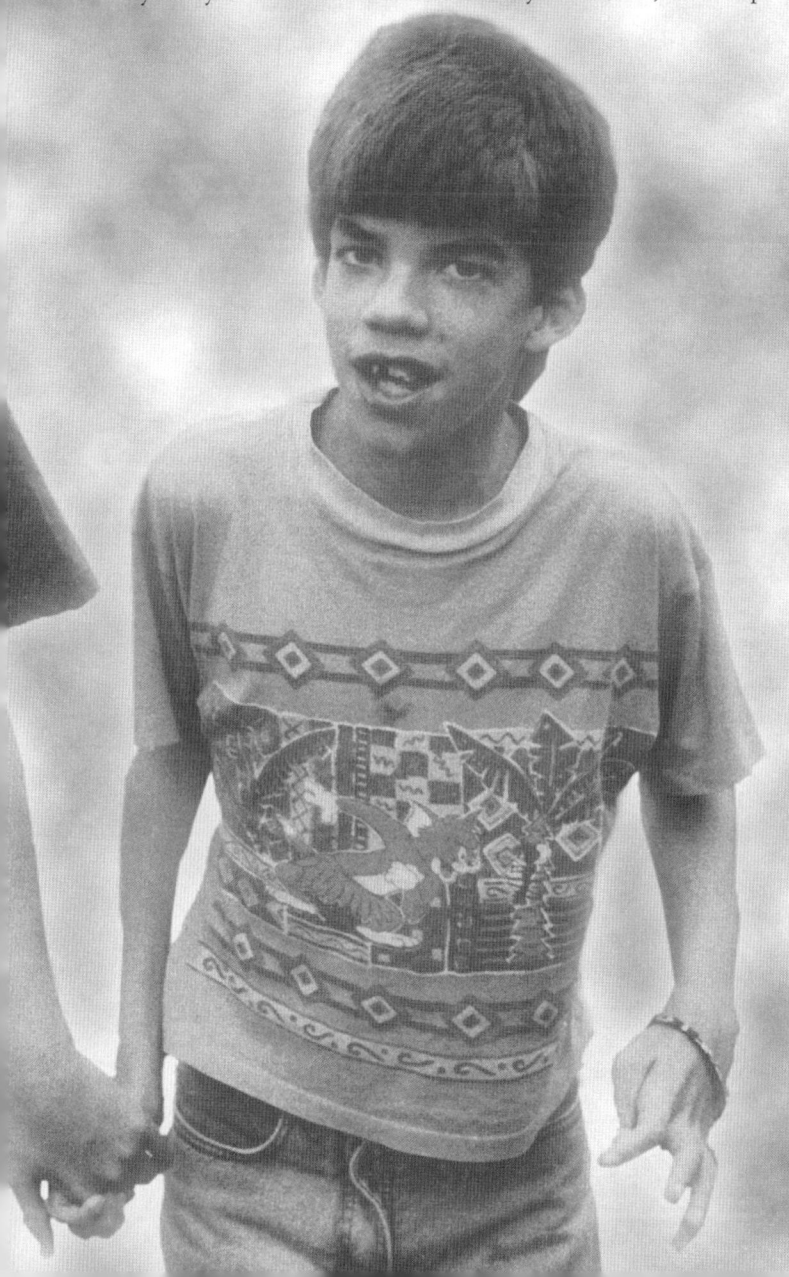

just your brother. You don't make him do things he doesn't want to do. You don't try and teach him any things he can't do. You just let him be. To be who he is without any questions asked.

Watching you and Kim be together has taught me. Being with you has taught me. Being with Kim has taught me.

And now you are teaching others the same lesson. Yesterday you came home from school saying you had had a nice conversation with one of your friends, M. You and M had been talking together when she suddenly said, "Jessie, I really love you."

"Oh yeah, and I really love you", you replied.

"No, I mean it. I really do love you. You are always so nice to people. You never say anything horrible. And look at the way you are with Kim. You don't treat him any different. I wish I could do that."

"Kim's my brother. I feel the same way about him as you do about your brother."

You are teaching M, and all your friends who spend time with you and Kim, the same lesson. You are teaching them to value being as opposed to doing. You teach in the best possible way – not by telling or by preaching but simply by being. You and Kim are living examples of the lesson.

Over the years many people who do not understand have pitied you for belonging to such an inadequate family.

"Poor Jessie, her mum's a single parent, her brother is disabled and needs so much attention – what a hard time she has."

You laugh light heartedly at such statements and say you would not change your family for the world.

"We are a perfect family", you say to me with your heart.

I look at you in awe, Jess, and wonder at the privilege I have in being your mother.

Pippa Murray

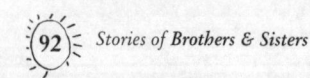

KIM

There's a light inside Kim - it's like a warm candle glowing. It's all orangey.

Sometimes the candle gets blown out and the warmth stops, but if you pay a bit of attention to him it comes back. Sometimes the light goes out when he is poorly, sometimes the light goes out when he is excluded. It glows most brightly when he is well and when he is at the centre of things.

Jessie Murray, his sister

" We dream for our children and for your children - for our children's children and for your children's children. We dream that children who are labelled, like our children are today, will one day be included without the slightest surprise, debate or controversy. "

SNAG Parents Group

Contributors to the Collection

Julie Dalton
Judith Gwynn
Matthew Gwynn
Simon Gwynn
Lindsay Hanson
George Hawkins
Pauline Hughes
Agnes Jenkinson
Joe Jenkinson
Paul Jenkinson
Sam Jenkinson
Graham Jones
Lily Jones
Stephen Jones
Caroline MacKeith
Maresa MacKeith
Julie Molloy
Val Molloy
Vince Molloy
Bethan Morgan
Norma Morgan
Sian Morgan
Freddy Morrison
Jessie Murray
Kim Murray
Pippa Murray
Jill Penman
SNAG Parents Group
Anne Williamson

We hope to continue to develop possibilities for story telling in the future. We can be contacted at:

ibk initiatives
Aizlewood's Mill
Nursery Street
Sheffield
S3 8GG

Email: info@ibkinitiatives.com
www.ibkinitiatives.com